Deconstructing Brazil

Beyond Carnival,

Soccer and

Girls in Small Bikinis

Simone Torres Costa

First Edition 2015

First Published in the United Kingdom by Springtime Books

© Copyright Simone Torres Costa

All rights reserved. No part of this publication may be reproduced, stored in or introduced into a retrieval system, or transmitted, in any form, or by any means (electronic, mechanical, photocopying recording or otherwise) without the prior written permission of the publisher.

This book is sold subject to the condition that it shall not, by way of trade or otherwise, be lent, resold, hired out, or otherwise circulated without the publisher's prior consent in any form of binding or cover other than that in which it is published and without a similar condition including this condition being imposed on the subsequent purchaser.

ISBN: 978-0-9932377-4-4

Cover design by Leigh Cann: lcann563@gmail.com

Acknowledgments

More than a book about Brazil, this was a journey to reconnect to and validate my own origins. I am grateful to my parents, Nilton Costa and Marines Torres, for the opportunities they created; to Richard Wagner, Luiz Izola, Berenice Camargo and Marisa Torres for their affection; and to Ulf Eriksson, Linus Axel Costa Eriksson and Sofia Clara Costa Eriksson for challenging me every day to find my real self and stick to it.

I am especially thankful to Rita de Cássia Chicarelli, Alexandra Paes Barreto and Eliene Leite for their unconditional friendship and support. I am also thankful for Renata Harper, my South African friend, who not only reviewed my writings but also instantly connected to them through the struggles our countries share.

My inspiration to look inwards for the missing pieces of Brazil would not have been possible without the genuine personal contributions of Andrea Borghi (anthropologist) and Edson Luis Gomes (archeologist), who embraced their passion fearlessly and shamelessly despite all the challenges they face in Brazil. When I grow up, I want to be like you.

Contents

Preface vi

Chapter 1: The Intercultural Movement 1

Chapter 2: Brazil Within Latin America 15

Chapter 3: The Invisible Influence 27

Chapter 4: A Case of Resilience 45

Chapter 5: The Colonial Legacy Today 63

Chapter 6: Leadership Skills in Brazil 75

Chapter 7: An Emerging Cultural Approach 91

Chapter 8: Epilogue 103

Glossary of Foreign Words 107

Bibliography 110

About the Author 121

Preface

During a recent trip to Sweden, my husband and I invited a friend, a well-known journalist, over for dinner and suggested he come visit Brazil. This is what he said: "Why would I risk my life, and my family's, to go to a country where I could be kidnapped or robbed on the street at any time?" Although his response was probably based on crime statistics and some undeniable facts about the reality of Brazilian society, a powerless feeling overtook me and blocked any attempt to come up with a reasonably good defence of Brazil's image (and consequently, my own image as a Brazilian).

During my intercultural training, psychology, and coaching practices, and as a Brazilian who has lived abroad for over 15 years (in the USA, Sweden, Poland and Italy), I have found myself too often explaining to non-Brazilians that, yes, Brazil is still a developing country (which comes with the indictment of being a former 'third world country') with enormous social gaps. Yet, there is more to the country than this – and there is certainly more to it than carnival, soccer, and girls in small bikinis. Discussions about Brazil have always taken plenty of energy and effort, as if I have had to defend myself and disprove what the international media chooses to portray about our people and culture(s). Once, during a business meeting in Europe, an Italian was surprised when she realized I was Brazilian. "Oh! I thought most Brazilians were black, as in your national soccer team," she said. This kind of comment shows a lack of social sensitivity, but it also shows how little information is required before our minds form a general picture of a country.

For many years my search for convincing arguments to validate my personal theory – that Brazil is much more than a paradise for criminals or sex tourists – was always accompanied by doubts. Often I thought to myself, *'Maybe it is easier to let people think whatever they want...*

maybe this superficial image of Brazil is not so bad after all. Indeed,' I wondered, *'who am I to change this?'* But one question kept coming back to me... It is probably the most important question that I have tried to answer in this book and it motivated my research:

What relevant information should be added to this superficial and incomplete picture of Brazil?

I needed to pinpoint exactly what foreigners (as well as Brazilians) should know that would make a qualitative difference to their understanding of such a complex culture. Hopefully, this knowledge could also enhance their ability to interact constructively with Brazilians. Interculturalists know that learning about country specifics – general information easily found online – is not sufficient for a person to develop an ability to deal with cultural differences. In order to develop what is called *intercultural competence*, people need to gather knowledge, but they also need to address skills, attitude, and awareness of the underlying values of a culture.

With this purpose in mind, I ventured into re-studying the history of Brazil, focusing on three key aspects:

- The factors which differentiate Brazil from the rest of Latin America.

- The long-lasting characteristics of our original peoples, the Native Brazilians or Amerindians, as well as those who followed; namely the Portuguese settlers ('the invaders'), and finally the Africans (our first 'forced immigrants').

- The imprinted intercultural dynamics of the early encounters between the Native Brazilians and the 'old settlers' (mainly the Portuguese and Africans), and what made this interaction so unique.

Having shed light on these key aspects would enable me to find and understand links between historic and socio-economic events and the Brazilian cultural behaviours of today. The more I read, however, the more I felt the need to emphasize, among other things, that the nature and intensity of those original tri-ethnic interactions (i.e. between the Amerindians, old settlers and Africans) influenced and structured our society long before the arrival of all other immigrants.

Even if this book does not focus on the interaction among the recent immigrant groups, it can help to explain why the relatively recent immigrants, such as Italians, Germans and even Japanese, have had more pressure on them to 'Brazilianize' rather than the other way around. Indeed, these immigrants were more influenced than expected by the culture that had already formed by the time they arrived.

Although the influence of these more recent immigrants is strong in isolated areas of Brazil, I have chosen to concentrate on the earlier interactions as I believe these are the missing pieces in our understanding of the Brazil of today. In my view, the early interactions and historical events have been underexplored and not taken seriously enough. Much has changed in the last 40 years, but I still advocate for the need to explore the root causes and deep, often subconscious, effects of the early interactions of the Brazilian culture. Just as early childhood events play a key role in every human being's formation, early interactions in a country's history will have a powerful and long-lasting influence.

For a more accurate picture of the Brazil of today, we must explore the fact that, in four out of the past five centuries of post-colonization, the main characters were almost exclusively the Brazilian Indians, the Portuguese and the Africans (with a few exceptions of early but limited contacts with the Dutch, English and French). Moreover, the historic events during this intense tri-cultural interaction were dominated by colonialism led by Catholic counter-reformers, and driven by slave commerce, political dependency on the motherland (Portugal), economic exploration and social inequality. The characteristics of this prolonged interaction have deeply influenced the values and attitudes submerged in the Brazilian *cultural iceberg* – a popular model used in intercultural trainings which explores both visible (behaviours, language) and invisible (values, beliefs) aspects of a culture. The iceberg model invites us to go deeper and can be used as the basis of any attempt to comprehend the more typical Brazilian behaviours and ways of living and working.

My initial focus was therefore to explore the intercultural elements and interpersonal challenges in the *formation* of Brazil, which I especially based on the work of writers Darcy Ribeiro, Katia M. de Queirós Mattoso, Celso Furtado and Frank Tannenbaum. Despite the criticism from my anthropologist friends, I agree with Ribeiro's anthropological masterpiece, *The Brazilian People: The Formation and Meaning of Brazil* (a key inspiration for this book), that the formation of a Brazilian national ethnic group/culture must be understood, first of all, from the interaction between these three groups, in a process he calls, "the Brazilian ethnic gestation". This will be discussed in more detail in *Chapter 3: The Invisible Influence*. Understanding this concept of *gestation* is essential to enlightening us about Brazil and invalidating the many myths surrounding the country. The general impression of Brazil as just another multicultural country, a 'melting pot', is not entirely correct. On the contrary, Brazil can be considered in many ways a 'hard to mix' multicultural society. The 'melting pot' description does not reveal much about *how* it all happened and lacks the (essential) differentiation between *old settlers* and *recent immigrants*.

In my search for answers, I soon realized that in order to honestly explain the Brazilian people, we must also further acknowledge two important factors: first, our history did not start five hundred years ago with the arrival of the Portuguese. And second, the influence of the indigenous population, the Amerindians, on the most common Brazilian values and behaviours was unique in size, intensity and nature – a process qualitatively different from colonies such as those in North America and Australia. Understanding their influence may even explain the most common behaviours of Brazilians at work (more in *Chapter 5: The Colonial Legacy Today*).

Note that whenever I use the word 'Brazilian', I include myself 100 percent of the time, whether it is a positive or negative reference. Throughout this book, however, I have tried to relate to the everyday cultural clashes experienced by my foreign clients and friends who, for business or personal reasons, live and work in Brazil. Of course, I am fully aware of the danger of over-generalizing nationalities, especially ones as heterogeneous as the Brazilian nation. I decided to take the risk, though, of unpacking cultural aspects of some behaviours believed to be 'typically Brazilian' because my objective is to constructively bring these into awareness. (My intention is neither to judge nor justify them.) By using a 'foreign eye', I could also explore the empathy necessary to go beyond judgments and stereotypes. Without having gone through the same everyday struggles myself in a foreign country, I could not have dared to write this book.

Furthermore, even though international experiences are more and more common, as a psychologist, I must also remember that the human brain is an outdated hardware to handle some intercultural challenges. Even with its great potential to learn and adapt, the brain has limited emotional and cognitive biases. Dealing with failures and conflicts within intercultural interactions remains a major challenge for us all; it is not surprising to find a gap between our knowledge about a country – information – and how well we handle differences and conflicts.

The speed of information, which flows around the globe in an instant, might give the impression that, sooner or later, national cultures will become uniform or even obsolete. The need to understand cultural differences, and deal with them in a constructive manner, becomes ever more important as intercultural interactions increase. The amount of information on culture available online is enormous. Failure in the true internationalization (of both individuals and companies) is not due to lack of information then, but rather due to lack of *intercultural sensitivity*, a 'soft skill', which goes beyond simplified historical knowledge.

The challenges and international conflicts faced by nations and multi-cultural organizations (particularly after mergers and acquisitions) continue, despite advances in information technology. These conflicts can be costly to businesses and nations, one of many reasons why it is essential for them to identify more precisely what is *cultural* about their problems.

As for individuals (especially those intending to cross the Brazilian border), in order to be successful they are similarly required to go beyond the often superficial geographic and historical information and to take into account challenges such as perception distortions, misleading expectations, miscommunication, and so on. The demand from individuals and organizations for an elaborated intercultural frame-work of the Brazilian culture, therefore, is still a valid one. For instance, according to McNulty (2012), estimates of 'employee premature return rate' in international assignments range from 16 to 61 percent; I have no reason to believe the rate for those working in Brazil would be any better.

The need to study the emerging countries from a new perspective, not only from a traditional Western/ Eurocentric point of view, persists especially after the recent economic global turnaround, which has seen the game changing. Emerging countries themselves have an important role to play in creating these alternative worldviews. This book is an attempt to offer an additional perspective to the dynamics of intercultural relations, and, specifically, to how foreigners tend to see the Brazilian culture (as well as how Brazilians see themselves). The information shown in the media about the Brazilian culture (or cultures) is usually incomplete, and lacks historical and contextual understanding.

In order to fill this gap this book takes a multidisciplinary approach – borrowing from anthropology, history and intercultural psychology – in exploring the Brazilian culture of today. The objective is to explain, but not necessarily to justify, some everyday Brazilian cultural behaviours commonly misunderstood by foreigners, such as the tendency of Brazilians to ignore time, our difficulty in saying "no", our love-hate relationship with foreigners, and finally the dynamics of 'the ugly' versus 'the beautiful' people in the Brazilian society.

Finally, although this is not intended to be a history book, it does aim to fill the glaring information gap that can create separation or division between Brazilians and foreigners (not to mention between the Brazilians' old and new image of themselves). It is not an academic book, but rather was born from my observation as an intercultural professional and, of course, as a Brazilian.

Above all, this book aims at guiding readers, interculturalists, business people, and those who want a deeper understanding of Brazil, to go beyond the superficial idea of Brazil as 'one big mixed culture'. By exploring some of the historical and anthropological aspects of the different original ethnic groups – and how they integrated and interacted – I also hope to explain some of the common Brazilian behaviours. Hopefully this book will also offer a framework for a better and more truthful cooperation between Brazilians and non-Brazilians, whether in business or in interpersonal interactions.

Chapter 1

The Intercultural Movement

Highlights

Culture is like the wind.

◆

Perception mechanisms and the limitations of the individual human mind shape our cultural experience.

◆

Where you are coming from and/ or where you are going to matter.

◆

The Intercultural Movement Model helps us to understand the Brazilian culture.

Chapter 1: The Intercultural Movement

A good starting point to our discussion about Brazil is to clarify the definition of *culture*, a concept that is 'fought over' by all social sciences disciplines. For some authors, *culture* does not really exist. Rather, we should focus on *individual personality* and *social context*, which, when combined, are better predictors of behaviour (Rana, 2014). He argues that we seem to blame *culture* when social interactions become difficult – yet when all is going smoothly, *culture* appears to disappear; it becomes irrelevant and we can finally focus on our human commonalities. From the psychological perspective though, culture, even if it is a fluid concept, is considered to be one of the mediators of behaviours. In fact, our brains start categorizing another's face (in terms of race, for instance) within one or two tenths of a second (Ito & Urland in Fiske & Taylor, 2013). Our conscious and unconscious categorizations trigger attitudes, stereotypes, and impact on social behaviours. Culture is always there.

Who we think we are (our individual and national identity in comparison to others), and how we perceive others, have an impact on our social effectiveness. Any foreigner crossing the border into Brazil, or facing any cross-cultural border for that matter, will benefit from understanding some basic psychological principles – more specifically, how *their nationality, where they are going* and *their attitude* impact the quality of interactions in the foreign land. My claim is that foreigners who are aware of their own attitude have a competitive edge in Brazil.

In this chapter I will elaborate on individual social awareness and on the 'soft skills' necessary to ease our struggle in dealing with cultural differences. Without such awareness and sensitivity, the Brazilian culture might seem like just another complicated high context culture (Hall, 1976), as interculturalists like to categorize it (cultures in which implicit communication and informal rules prevail). By the end of the chapter, I promise to have made the relevant connections to help the reader succeed in building personal and professional relationships in Brazil.

One of my favorite analogies is, "Culture is like the wind" (McIver, 1926), on which I further elaborate to support the idea of culture being a fluid concept. When we look out of the window, how do we know it is a windy day? As the wind is invisible to our eyes, we look rather for its impact on our environment, on our senses and subjectivities. We might see the branches of the trees bending; we might hear the rustle of the wind through the leaves. If we step outside, we might feel the wind on our skin... So these manifestations confirm it is a windy day. Like the wind, culture is intangible; its manifestations demonstrate its nature and characteristics. Culture is one of the key factors underlying *behaviour*. Depending on what people are used to, and where they come from, the wind (to continue our analogy) can provoke positive or negative sensations and feelings. For some, the wind is welcome and refreshing; for others, it may be intrusive and disturbing, and they might prefer to step inside again. It is important to bear in mind that one person's interpretation or perception might be different to that of another, even though they have sensed (seen and heard) the same stimulus.

This simplistic explanation works best though for a *homogeneous* culture, such as the Swedish culture, in which all visible signs (behaviour, words, customs) lead to only one or a few interpretations. Often the intangible and invisible characteristics of one culture (such as values and beliefs) mislead us into a perception of 'one culture', when in fact there are many *levels* of cultures: the national, the regional, the ethnic, the family, the individual and particularly the socio-economic level. This misperception of 'one culture' is certainly the case for Brazil (and other high context cultures such as India and China) and is disturbing not only because of the country's ethnic diversity, but also because a rigid socio-economic stratification was created within this complex society. The heterogeneous aspects of the Brazilian culture can therefore be confusing, especially from a foreigner's perspective.

Any discussion of culture carries some interesting challenges, for culture is dynamic (it is constantly being socially constructed) and fully subjected to the perception mechanisms of the individual human mind. These *perception mechanisms* are influenced by a person's previous experiences, preconceptions and expectations. Furthermore, no matter which culture we are referring to, we can only deal with its manifestations (such as language, customs and cultural behaviours), not with the culture itself. If we take seriously that perceptions of another culture depend to a large extent on a person's previous knowledge (information from the media for example) and international exposure, we arrive at another interesting concept – also relevant to our discussion – which I call the *intercultural movement model*.

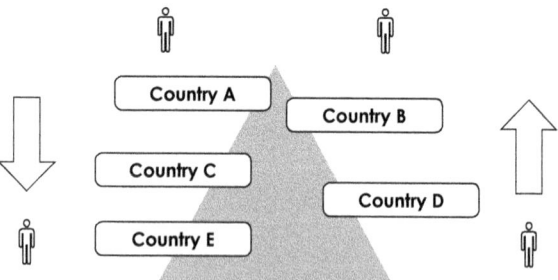

Fig 1. The Intercultural Movement Model

The general idea of this model is to show how *attitude towards nationality* impacts on our identity, stereotyping, and the quality of intercultural interactions. Foreigners working in Brazil often become accepted (or not) based on their attitude. As I will explain later in this chapter, Brazilians are very sensitive to the non-verbal and implicit impressions of foreigners. A basic understanding of the power of one's embodied attitude can make a real difference in dealing with the Brazilian culture.

First of all we must acknowledge that we live in a hierarchical international context in which nations are categorized into unequal social economic positions. People normally use the human development index (HDI), or categories such as *developed, developing or underdeveloped* countries, to describe these social structural differences.

From a psychological perspective, these basic categorizations play an important role in social interactions. An individual's social identity has to do – among other things – with group memberships such as nationality. Tajfel and Turner's theory of social identity (1979, 1986 cited in Coleman, et al., 2012) and the associated self-categorization theory (Turner, 1982, 1985, 2004 cited in Coleman, et al., 2012) suggest that these memberships are fundamental to the self, providing both a sense of belonging and a sense of distinctiveness. Also, social identity influences one's perception of others and one's behaviour. In other words, any intercultural encounter between two individuals hides a deeper level of interaction between two socio-economic realities, which is brought by them through their national identity. These national identities become relevant especially when compared to each other.

The Role of Nationality

Any time we go outside of our national borders, we bring our national identity and, consciously or unconsciously, a fixed hierarchy of the socio-economic development of countries. This hierarchy is based on perceptions gleaned from general information, usually from the media; the values attributed to this information; and historical and political power dynamics. In other words, we tend to initially categorize countries and their nationals according to this hierarchy. As a consequence, our minds have a tendency to place countries (and their nationals) in a lower or higher position relative to our own country or people, again confirming our ethnocentric viewpoint. This occurs even when there is a lack of detailed information available to us and even if clues to the positions of each country within the hierarchy are vague or incomplete. In this way our opinions about, and expectations of, other cultures are easily constructed in our minds. These perceptions may be false, but until we receive more information that confirms or changes them, they are stable enough to influence our behaviour (Gigerenzer, 2007).

Another crucial aspect of any social dynamic is revealed through two instinctive questions: "Is the other party an ally or a threat?" and "How capable and friendly is he/ she?"; that is, evaluations based on *competence* and *warmth*. These basic concerns have evolutionary origins and can help us understand many unconscious, automatic categorization, and stereotyping processes. The first question helps us decide whether or not to trust the other person. The issue of trust is very relevant to the Brazilian culture and will be specifically discussed in *Chapter 6: Leadership Skills in Brazil*. The second question, regarding how competent and friendly we perceive others to be, is very much associated with nationality. Cuddy et al.'s (2009) research into the original 15 countries of the European Union showed that nationals from these countries evaluate themselves and others based on the qualities of *competence* and *warmth*. The less developed South European countries such as Portugal and Spain, are perceived as *warmer*, but *less competent* than the more developed countries such as Germany and the United Kingdom. And those from the Central European and Nordic countries are perceived by South Europeans as *less warm* and *more competent*. The authors discuss the ideal characteristics of being *warm and competent* as a driving model, but it is likely to be an imaginary perception. It seems to be clear that, in general, not only do we classify other nationals as 'better or worse', but we also make an even deeper evaluation about their competence and warmth.

Acknowledging how different nationalities are perceived depending on their socio-economic position in the hierarchy can help us explain many of the challenges of intercultural relations. It also helps us place Brazil in this hierarchical context. By doing this, we can also investigate what happens when people move up and down as they cross borders (cultural or national), and how this movement, and the attitudes associated with it, impact on the quality of the intercultural interactions.

In summary, there are some implications of people's perceptions of each other – and their position in the socio-economic hierarchy – that affect the quality of their interactions:

1. Our mind goes beyond the information available and 'fills in' the gaps. "Carnival, soccer, girls in small bikinis… sounds like a very warm culture – but maybe they are not very competent." Judgments like this might occur no matter the amount and quality

of the informationwe receive. In an intercultural context the mind tends to make a quick evaluation about other countries and categorize them (and their nationals) as 'superior' or 'inferior' to our own (and to others).

2. Any judgment is highly subjective. Whenever we judge someone, there will be an impact on our expectations and how we communicate. Our judgments are not always based on 'facts', (they rarely represent the whole truth), but they nonetheless have the potential to influence our behaviour – unless (or until) it becomes conscious.

3. When moving 'up' to a more developed country, those from countries in a perceived lower position usually share similar experiences. This is true for lower ranked countries from different continents: when Asians and Latin Americans meet in Europe, they understand each other and share the difficulties of being 'someone from a less developed country' in Europe. In the Italian language there is the phrase *extra communitari*, or those who come from outside the European Community – a good example of an explicit *linguistic* categorization. This kind of categorization can suggest that belonging to the 'community' means belonging to the same group but ignores the many differences within it.

4. Similarly, people from countries categorized in a higher position in the socio-economic hierarchy share similar intercultural experiences when moving to a country of a perceived lower position, or dealing with its people. For example, an Australian and Norwegian living in Colombia might share the same kind of experience; namely being from a more developed country and living in a less developed one.

Cultural Boundaries

Defining who we are (and compared to whom) are central issues in any social interaction. We continuously evaluate who we are (and who we are not), consciously and unconsciously, in relation to others. But what is the boundary separating the in-group (we) and the out-group (they)? This borderline is often fragile and subtle but it plays an important role. From an anthropological perspective, the study of the *boundary maintaining process* by the anthropologist Fredrik Barth (1995) supports the argument that, first of all, there is a dynamic evaluation in relation to others that determines the collective identity; indeed categorizations are frequently based on the 'dichotomized statuses' of better or worse, superior or inferior. Secondly, the author recognizes that cultural boundaries can persist despite interactions across them.

The commonly used term *cross-cultural* in the modern intercultural literature relates to *boundary*, the borderline between cultures. In this sense it serves a function in the *identity process*. According to Barth (1995), it is "boundary that defines the group, not the cultural stuff that it encloses." Other authors prefer the term *difference* as a more appropriate term than boundary (Emberling, 1997). Either way, the study of the movement across borders is believed to contribute to our understanding of cultural interactions because it emphasizes that national identities take form in relation to other national identities and according to how they are perceived. In the case of migrations such as the Afro-American, Asian American and Hispanic peoples within the United States, the *shared experience of movement* (and isolation) enhances their sense of unity (Emberling, 1997). As we will discuss in *Chapter 2: Brazil Within Latin America*, the idea of intercultural movement will also help explain the dynamics of the Brazilian national identity within Latin America.

Attitudes in Brazil

Having the right attitude is obviously important in any human interaction. Having the right attitude in Brazil, and in other high context emerging countries, is more important for a number of reasons. Verbal and written communications in those countries are not so relevant. Implicit and *indirect communication*, which includes all contextual, subjective and non-verbal impressions and embodied attitudes, tends to be much more intense. It is as if Brazilians have an extra antenna picking up non-verbal signals, which will be used to interpret the *real intentions* behind what is being said. In the Brazilian culture, as we will explore in the next chapters, people have to constantly interpret particularities of the social classes, ethnicity and educational background differences in order to validate (or not) the *explicit communication*. My North American and North European clients usually have to be reminded to 'grow' this extra antenna to be able to know what Brazilians mean when they say, "Yes, let's meet up later". (Is this just something they say to be nice or do they really mean it?)

Besides finding a common pattern in the experience and expectations of those moving down or moving up the socio-economic hierarchy, the intercultural movement model can also help us pinpoint constructive or destructive attitudes; the latter might even lead to conflict. In this book, the term *attitude* will be defined as equivalent to the definition of the term *psychological orientation* (PO): "a consistent pattern of cognitive, motivational, moral and action orientation that guides one's behavior and responses" (Deutsch 2007, 2011 cited in Coleman et al., 2012). In other words, attitude consists of all the beliefs and ideas one has about a specific nationality. Attitude intermediates between a stimulus (nationality) and potential behaviour (Fiske & Taylor, 2013). Our attitude can be implicit or explicit; either way, it will influence how we interact with others.

I must confess it was a relief to read these explanations of attitude and perception in my psychology books, because it leant academic weight to how I have experienced and witnessed intercultural relations since I first left Brazil 27 years ago. When individuals are under stress, during conflicts, or in situations of personal or professional confrontations, we seem to bring out our differences even more. Even if social conflict is a fact of life and the "basic driver of human development" (Coleman et al., 2012), it is challenging because it usually underlies opposing goals, claims, beliefs, values, etc. In these situations of perceived power imbalance, it is common for individuals to take the position of either *dominance* or *victimization* – according to the Situated Model of Conflicts in Social Relations by Coleman et al., (2012).

Perceived inferiority and superiority are associated with attitudes of *arrogance and intimidation* respectively, and both attitudes have a direct impact on communication, conflict resolution and group/individual performance, especially within organizations. This might explain why the performance of international teams who have not received proper intercultural coaching and training can be adversely affected (as researched by Martha Mazlevski, professor at the International Institute of Management MBA programs). Indeed, prevalent attitudes of this nature interfere with, and may hinder, intercultural understanding and cooperation. Both attitudes are more common in people with limited international exposure, and tend to decrease as people become more interculturally sensitive. This is beautifully explained by Milton Bennett (1993 and 2004) in his *Developmental Model of Intercultural Sensitivity* (DMIS). As we become more interculturally competent, we learn to value the subtle skills of human interactions.

Implications for the Brazilian culture

How specifically do the concepts of *culture*, or *intercultural movement*, relate to our discussion about the Brazilian culture? Firstly, despite the latest economic crisis and the consequent changes in the global (socio-economic) hierarchy of countries, there are still many preconceived ideas and stereotypes about Brazil. Brazilians are particularly sensitive to how they are perceived by foreigners due to, among other factors, the long-lasting social and economic rule of outsiders (the colonizers) and the country's lack of autonomy in that time. This aspect of history is shared with many other former colonies that have not yet reached high levels of development. The social dynamics during colonization endure and are imprinted in our collective mind. This could be seen as part of the "the psychology of colonialism" (Mannoni, 1991), characterized by the relationship of 'dependence' between colonialists, who play an active role, and the colonized 'primitive' people who play a passive role. Further support for this argument will be explored in *Chapter 4: A Case of Resilience, Chapter 5: The Colonial Legacy Today* and *Chapter 6: Leadership Skills in Brazil.*

Secondly, Brazil (like other emerging countries) is by nature *volatile, uncertain, complex and ambiguous* (VUCA) – a now popular business term. This is especially true in relation to its *own uncertainty* over national identity, and its wavering self-esteem. Even if there are no 'stable' national identities anywhere, this seems to be an especially sensitive discussion among many Brazilians. Brazilians (including myself) are often asked one of the most embarrassing questions: how such a large country so rich in natural resources can be so socially underdeveloped – especially in comparison to former colonies such as the US and Australia? How can we be so behind in terms of technology, education, health systems? ... we all wonder. Brazilians do not seem to have come to terms with this question. This is, however, deep within the core of our 'unsolved' identity, which will be discussed in the following chapters. The question, *"What happened to us that we became so socio-economically behind?"* is more commonly asked than, *"What have we done and not done to let this happen?"* It's as if we are still not sure and cannot pinpoint what went wrong.

Historians, anthropologists and economists have offered many explanations, including the religion of the colonizers. The Portuguese counter-reform Catholicism, when compared to Protestantism, represents a less pragmatic, less rational approach to colonization. Celso Furtado, a well-known economist and expert on the economic formation of Brazil, offers his views based on the types of large-scale economic activities predominant for centuries in Brazil. As we will discuss later, large-scale economic activities (such as sugar cane and coffee plantation) are believed to increase social inequalities. Blaming isolated past events is obviously not very useful. The answer likely lies in a combination of factors, some of which will be discussed in the next chapters.

Deciding where Brazil is socio-economically is still a popular topic of conversation in Brazil – a question that remains unanswered – and it is probably the central theme in the construction of a more 'settled' national identity. Schwarcz (1993) describes it as an uncomfortable topic becoming a "local obsession" at times. Perhaps as a result of this dilemma – which can also be understood as an 'inferiority complex' – Brazilians keep comparing ourselves and look up to North Americans and Europeans in general in order to define where we are. *They must have something we do not*, the thinking goes. *They must be better, richer, 'whiter', taller, more educated, etc.* In general, Brazilians also look up to these nations not only for what they bring, but also because of who we think they are.

Due to centuries of economic restrictions, as well as the 19th century protectionism to benefit local industries (imposed by the government until 1988), the Brazilian economy has been isolated. Import taxes were so high at one stage that imported consumer goods in Brazil were non-existent; anything imported came (mostly illegally) from Paraguay. By making importation economically unviable, these protectionist policies also postponed access to international goods and professional exchanges. As a consequence, Brazilian society stagnated and had little international contact until the late 1980s. To travel abroad and to own a pair of Nike tennis shoes were exclusive to the (very) rich elite. The low level of income and purchasing power of the general population – until two decades ago – limited exposure to international markets. It also restricted international relations, as most people could not afford basic consumer goods, never mind a trip abroad.

As national industry became obsolete and government focused only on internal chronic economic crisis, Brazil became (economically) irrelevant in the international arena. The educational gap between the majority of Brazilians and the 'developed' world (discussed in more detail in *Chapter 6: Leadership Skills in Brazil*) also leads the average Brazilian to think of foreigners (West Europeans and North Americans in particular) as 'superior', which partially explains the underestimated national identity. The relationship between economics and national identity is not a simple one (and it is one of the challenges faced by anthropologists). My impression, though, is that it deeply impacts our perception of where we are in comparison to others.

Our collective self-esteem has recently improved, however, with the return of Brazilians who had emigrated during the 1980s to escape high inflation and unemployment; the elimination of import/ export restrictions; and the recent economic development that has increased international exposure of Brazil. Nonetheless, this new Brazilian national pride seems to fluctuate wildly and building it is an ongoing process. Indeed, our national pride appears to move up and down with the stock market, GDP growth, and other economic results – in psychology we call this *performance-based self esteem*. The latest test was our performance in organizing and hosting the FIFA World Cup (2014) – the Rio Olympic Games (2016) will be the new test. "Are we capable enough?" is the agonizing question being asked in most Brazilian political and social gatherings. It is as if the Brazilian national identity hangs on the success of these events. I believe this fear of a potential collective failure will continue to have an impact in the years to come on how Brazilians take responsibility in making the social changes necessary.

Our national identity only seems to be stable and confident when we are talking about our neighbor Argentina. This is obviously a joke. But as with any good joke there is always a serious point being made. During an intercultural workshop in which there were Brazilian and Argentinean participants, among other nationalities, I tried the following 'experiment':

- I asked the Brazilians: "If Brazil is country D in the pyramid (see Fig 1), where would you place Argentina?"

- I asked the Argentineans: "If Argentina is country D in the pyramid, where would you place Brazil?"

Even though Brazil and Argentina belong to Latin America and face relatively similar socio-economic struggles, both Brazilians and Argentineans placed the other as Country E (below). As mentioned earlier, behind socio-economic hierarchy theory lies the belief that people are not the same; the belief that the hierarchic position one (is thought to) occupy demonstrates one's intrinsic value in relation to others (superior or inferior in the dimensions of competence and warmth).

A Love-Hate Relationship

Brazilians seem to have a conflicting relationship with foreigners, a 'love-hate relationship'. This conflicting relationship reminds me of the early interactions between the native peoples and the Portuguese – the 'typical historical outsider' (this concept will be discussed in more detail in the following chapters). In the first reaction to a foreigner there is curiosity and openness; this is followed by an uncertainty as to whether this foreigner is 'just another *gringo*'. Each detail of the subsequent behaviours on the part of the foreigner will either reinforce or refute the original idea of the typical historical outsider. Even in business, the way foreign managers interact with Brazilians in terms of expectations and communication, and especially how they handle mistakes and delays, will determine what they will receive in return (more on the business culture in Brazil can be found in *Chapter 6: Leadership Skills in Brazil*). In intercultural encounters, when two unfamiliar realities meet, there are usually many deep and unconscious memories that may frame individuals' reactions to each other. Perceiving someone as an outsider brings back historical connotations; these were imprinted early on in Brazilian history and can have a concrete impact on doing business in Brazil.

This intense love-hate dynamic is also known as the *concept of dual attitudes* (Baumeister & Bushman, 2008), referring to the fact that the mind can have two different evaluations of the same object/ person. These conflicting evaluations can be implicit *and* explicit, and they can be changed according to the perceiver's motivation, or if challenged. In other words, we love foreigners because we have an idealized vision of them, but we quickly hate them at any sign of criticism.

The discussions in this chapter have hopefully helped the reader to realize that our worldview is based on socio-economic factors and is 'triangular' rather than global. The next chapters support the idea that we ought, perhaps, to deconstruct the ideas we have about Brazil. Telling my clients only about the history and geography of Brazil was not enough to have a real impact on their experience in Brazil. I knew there was something deeper which could make a significant difference and it lay in their self-awareness and attitudes.

Chapter 2
Brazil within Latin America

Highlights

Brazilians do not quite see themselves according to the American definition of 'Latinos'.

◆

The cultural distance between the Spanish and Portuguese colonies goes far beyond a language difference.

◆

Early colonial events and geography had an impact on the development of differences and similarities in Latin America.

Chapter 2: Brazil within Latin America

Looking into Latin America from the outside, most people will recognize this area as the immense continent on which the Spaniards and Portuguese put into practice their colonization skills and styles, and where the consequences of their successful (and unsuccessful) political and ideological choices remain. In our attempt to understand the Brazilian culture, it is essential to situate Brazil in its *regional* context. The similarities and differences among the native peoples from east to west and from north to south, as well as the differences in the colonization processes they were subjected to, are imprinted in what we see today in Latin America.

Florida, where I lived in the late 1980s, can be considered a living Latin American intercultural laboratory. Since that time I have been intrigued by the fact that Brazilians do not feel we fit the American definition of 'Latinos'. This has been a difficult, often shameful, thing to explain to my fellow Latin Americans. We do not feel better or worse, we just feel different. On one side, we all share the same South American continent with its colonial history and socio-economic difficulties; on the other, there is *something else* which makes our national identity somehow apart from this 'Latin American identity' as a whole, and which goes beyond our different languages (mainly Portuguese and Spanish).

The Socratic's humble approach that, "all we know, is that we know nothing" applies well in our attempt to study the circa 12,000 year history of Latin America. What we mostly know today is based on the biased Eurocentric written history of the last 500 years. Little is known in terms of non-written cultural and ecological knowledge of the native people (this theme will be further explored in the next chapter). The tendency to generalize and simplify the Latin American cultures into a few workable dimensions – for example, as *hierarchic, collectivist* (Hofstede, 2005) – limits our intercultural understanding when this is done in isolation and without further historical context. As has been touched upon briefly (and will be discussed further in *Chapter 6: Leadership Skills in Brazil*), many of the emergent countries, such as Brazil, India and China, can be categorized as being hierarchic, collectivist and high context; so too can most Latin American countries. Yet as we will soon see, a major difference between the Brazilian culture and many of the Spanish-speaking Latin American cultures exists around hierarchy and how people relate to power distance in the work environment – for example, what employees expect from their superiors. What, then, does this say about our intercultural categorization methods?

A more complete approach to the study of the Latin American cultures must consider the early historical context and especially the power imbalance of colonialism and its impact on social dynamics. My intention in this chapter, therefore, is mainly to:

- Emphasize the general similarities and differences (including development stages) between the diverse *native* cultures of Latin America, and how differently they interacted with the Spanish and Portuguese colonizers;

- Explore the impact of certain historical events in Spanish and Portuguese colonies that can help us better understand the regional differences.

The original Latin American peoples populating the region in 1492, when the first settlers made contact, probably sat between 35 and 55 million (Burkholder & Johnson, 2012). Although the Mayas, Aztecs and Incas are the civilizations best known from the age of conquest, the inhabitants of these empires constituted only a minority of the total Amerindian population and in only a small portion of Latin America's landscape. Aymara, Caribs, Chichimecas, Ge, Guaraní, Mapuche, Muisca, Otomí, Pueblo, Quibaya, Taino, Tepaneca, Tupí and Zapotec are just some of the other peoples that inhabited the Americas at this time. According to Burkholder and Johnson, they formed a "human mosaic whose diverse characteristics greatly influenced the way in which colonial Latin America developed". Having acknowledged that, this question comes to mind: how can we continue to ignore and put into one category all the indigenous populations – over 350 major tribal groups, 15 distinct cultural centers, and more than 160 linguistic stocks – which could be found in Latin America by 1500?

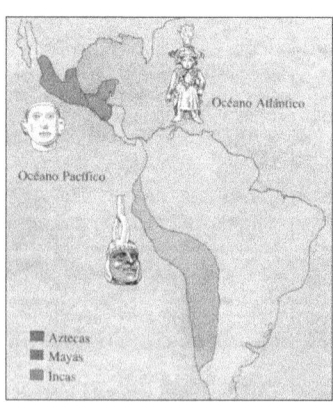

Fig 2. An overview of earlier civilizations of Latin America reveals only those commonly known to the West (source unknown)

The vast diversity among the native peoples makes a significant difference in the cultural formation of this continent yet is seldom acknowledged. Instead, we seem only to give importance to those civilizations who constructed impressive buildings and magnificent temples, namely those who had developed urban areas such as the Mayans, Aztecs and Incas, the 'civilized' societies of Mesoamerica and west Latin America. Their legacy in the construction of bridges and roads is remarkable. Historians call them 'high cultures'. The other ethnic groups, who were semi-sedentary or nomadic in South America and whose legacies do not include material accumulation or constructions, do not usually get our attention or respect. This is definitely the case for the ethnic groups in the vast territory of what is today, Brazil. That the semi-nomadic Brazilian indigenous population did not have any 'impressive' buildings made them 'primitive' in the eyes of the Portuguese invaders. The nature of their semi-nomadic societies, their social dynamics, and knowledge of the environment, however, became essential to the subsequent colonial development. (*Chapter 3: The Invisible Influence* will discuss the invisible impact these aspects have on the Brazilian culture.)

Similarities

All Latin Americans experienced the consequences of Iberian colonialism – mainly the approach of the Castellan and Portuguese Crowns – and experienced the effects of certain individuals' drive to maintain wealth and power through the use of violence and subjugation (the isolated cases of contact with the French, Dutch and English will not be discussed here). The social order in both Iberian empires in the 16th century was hierarchical with power, wealth and status concentrated at the top. "They neither believed in human equality nor had any enthusiasm for promoting social mobility," write Burkholder and Johnson (2012). Colonies existed merely to increase the economic well-being and political strength of the mother country. Their production and markets were intended to benefit solely Portugal and Spain (this is why sugar plantation and mining became the main economic activities for a couple of centuries). Both motherlands in turn regulated everything from trade to taxes in order to transfer wealth back to them.

Thus all Latin Americans share this *dualistic social process*: the white man's 'superiority' (and he equipped with weapons and tools) versus the native's primitive 'inferiority'. Furthermore, Latin Americans share experiences around an uneven relationship with the colonizers, who became an idealized reference point. In this relationship there was no real *cultural exchange*, in which two different cultures with similar power share respect; rather, there was *cultural appropriation* in which power inequality is the core element of social interactions and disintegration prevails. One of the consequences of such social dynamics is that the *ideology of inequality* is so deeply rooted it becomes the (social) norm. The political ideology and strategies that followed over the next 500 years mirror the idea that people in society are not equal; this prevalence of inequality remains evident today in an, "it's okay, this is who we are" attitude. This seems to be an ongoing process from east to west in Latin America, independent of the intensity of the ethnic miscegenation (or racial mixing).

All Latin American societies struggled to incorporate the white Iberian elite's materialist values, their tendency towards corrupt administration, their ideas of land ownership, and their search for gold and silver. Latin Americans also share the influence of the Iberian medieval pride in Christianity, which collides loudly with the essence of our spiritual ancestry worship. Even though Christianity grew, the belief in the supernatural and in the ancestors was widespread throughout the continent. Most of all, the Latin American countries have in common the same patterns of social interactions based on kinship, or tight family relations.

Differences

Although the Spaniards and the Portuguese had more or less the same objectives in 'the New World', their previous experience with dealing with other peoples appears to have differed. The Portuguese contact with the Moors and other African peoples in the 15th century seemed to make them more accustomed than the Spanish to mixing and inter-acting with other groups (Burkholder & Johnson, 2012).

The main strategy of the (Spanish) *conquistadores* was to approach the natives with force and violence, justified by their crown's eagerness to extract gold – found very early on 'the Spanish side' of the continent. This tactic may have been influenced by the Spaniards dealing with a more settled population and better organized groups (such as the Incas, Aztecs and Mayas) with a history of warfare. These native groups had previously abandoned the nomadic life, developing agriculture techniques and also becoming more hierarchic than those semi-nomadic groups settled on 'the Portuguese side'. In the Inca society, for example, there were usually five clear social layers: the *sapa Inca* or emperor, governor, local ruler, leader of household and commoner. This difference in hierarchy structures between the Portuguese and

Spanish sides, I believe, still has an impact today and ultimately on how much power distance (the distance between hierarchical levels) is accepted or not – even in the work environment. When I coach Mexican executives working in Brazil, for example, there are often different expectations of boss-subordinate relationships as well as the role of women in society. From a Brazilian perspective gender relations and hierarchy at work, as practiced by some of our neighbors, appear very rigid and traditional.

In general, even though most indigenous populations in the Spanish Latin America lacked iron and hard metal tools, with the exception of a small amount of bronze used by the Inca, they were politically organized in relatively egalitarian structures (certainly compared to western civilization of the time), whereby leaders were elected and advised by the elderly.

The social organization and hierarchical difference of the native peoples between the Portuguese and Spanish territories resulted in differences in how they tried to resist the Iberian invasion. Although there was violence on both sides, the more hierarchic, organized natives were able to mobilize and fought bitterly against the Spaniards before finally giving up their treasures. The Spaniards had a specific commodity to fight for: gold. The Portuguese, on the other hand, did not. The extraction of Brazil wood, which became a valuable commodity, required instead the help and collaboration of the indigenous groups. As a consequence the Portuguese used a 'softer' approach than the Spanish invaders; besides, the native groups on the Brazilian side were less prepared for wars. Very early on the Portuguese realized that violence was not particularly effective; they become instead 'part of' the indigenous family to gain the family's trust, through taking concubines and through 'hiring' voluntary labour (this topic will be further explored in the next chapter).

The Physical Distance

The aforementioned distance between the Brazilian identity and other 'Latinos' can also be explained by the actual physical distance between the initial regions of colonization and the hydrographic characteristics of the continent. The Spanish arrived mainly from the Caribbean and moved downwards to the southwest of Latin America, while the Portuguese arrived and populated the eastern coast. The geographic barriers between the colonizers at the time consisted not only of sheer distance and dense jungle areas, but also the nature of

South American rivers: most do not flow from east to west (or vice versa) and rather flow from the north Amazon region to the south (although the Amazon River starts in Peru and goes toward the Atlantic, it is surrounded by dense forests). An exception is the Parana River/ Las Plata River in the south, an area where the Portuguese and Spanish crowns (and the Church) did fight for territory. However, even here there has always been a relatively limited movement of people between the Spanish and Portuguese sides.

Communication and Cultural Exchange

Limited communication between the Spanish colonies and Brazil also maintained the distance between the two sides. The main channel of communication was between the colonies and its mother country and not much occurred between colonies, especially not between the Portuguese and Spanish sides. This was perpetuated by lack of communications and technologies, but it was also due to strategy. For example, the Portuguese Crown would have no interest in allowing news about the Haitian revolution to reach Brazil, lest it motivate local slaves to also fight for their rights. Information was restricted and tightly controlled, as was regional cooperation. In a colonized continent this was one of the political tactics of the Spanish and Portuguese Crowns to keep control over their colonies. As a consequence, the elite in the colonies tended to look up to the mainland as their only reference for education, ideology, fashion, art and history; they rarely looked to each other.

Limited communication inevitably resulted in limited cultural exchange between Brazil and other Latin American countries. Through the years this situation has improved; however, it remains inadequate to fill in the historical gaps. Recent attempts at regional economic integration, such as Mercosur, which started with Brazil, Argentina, Paraguay and Uruguay (and later included other neighboring countries), are still not cohesive enough to be effective, due to political weakness. Mercosur's primary focus – regional commercial integration – is rather narrow and emphasizes the exchange of goods; it does not explicitly include deeper educational and cultural exchange. The exchange we see happening (slowly) today between Brazil and the rest of Latin America remains superficial and is not as comprehensive as one would expect from regional neighbors. This project of regional integration, which was designed in theory long before the integration of the European Union, has had its challenges. During my school years in Brazil we studied the history of Europe, but never the history of our neighboring countries; the same was true for art, literature, music, etc. We will discuss education in Brazil (or the lack of it) in *Chapter 5: The Colonial Legacy Today*, but for now it is worth emphasizing that a regional identity is not fully experienced or shared due to the lack of exchange and cooperation among Latin American government and educational institutions – this despite the recent attempts by Mercosur.

The Spanish versus Portuguese Colonial Administration

The closer we look the more differences we find between the Spanish and Portuguese sides of the continent. Spanish colonial administration efforts started in the early 1500s. In contrast, administrative efforts in Brazil started intensively only in 1808, when the Portuguese Crown moved to Brazil to escape Napoleon's invasion of Portugal. It is clear that the nature and scope of political administration in their colonies differed vastly between the two Iberian powers.

Firstly, the distance between the Spanish colonies and Spain, and resultant delays in communication, were larger than those between Brazil and Portugal. The inland locations of Mexico and Bogota, where heavy gold mining was present, added extra travel time to the Iberian Peninsula (Burkholder & Johnson, 2012). A fleet sent from Spain to the Indies usually returned 14 to 15 months later, while the coastal location of all Brazil's major cities facilitated easier logistics and communication between the territory and Portugal. Secondly, the Spanish Crown discovered gold almost as soon as they arrived and this demanded immediate investment into establishing a system to closely control the transportation of this very valuable commodity – as well as the collection of taxes, for the indigenous populations too were required to pay these.

The presence of densely populated and advanced settled civilizations on the Spanish side led the Spanish Crown, from as early as 1535, to fully develop their administrative organization in a more intense and decentralized manner in order to deal with legislative, judicial, commercial, military and ecclesiastical matters (Burkholder & Johnson, 2012). On the other side, the Portuguese administration was more centralized due to the shorter distance to Portugal. However, prior to the royal family's arrival in 1808, administrative efforts were limited to developing logistics to export the main goods (sugar cane, and later, gold and diamonds) and tax collection. Investments into improving the citizens' quality of life (city infrastructure, schools, transport, etc.) started much later in the colony.

One of the implications of this differing administrative approach to the colonies was the difference in intensity and nature of investment into establishing universities and government institutions. The Spanish Crown established the first university in the New World (in Santo Domingo, the capital of Dominic Republic) in 1528. They also founded the Council of the Indies and sent administrative bodies – men with university training in civil or canon law – to the new institutions. In Brazil the first academy (a military academy) only arrived in 1808, in Bahia, almost three centuries later. Another century later (and four centuries after the first university on the Spanish side), in 1909, the University of Manaus was officially established. In 1911 came the University of São Paulo and in 1912 the University of Paraná.

This educational gap between the Spanish and the Portuguese colonies is a reflection of the lack of long-term interest the Portuguese had in the Brazilian society (even though they did care about its profitability). This continues to have profound consequences for the Brazil of today. We will discuss this further in *Chapter 5: The Colonial Legacy Today*.

Subsistence versus Economies of Scale

As mentioned earlier, the early discovery of gold and silver on the Spanish side of Latin America, and its relatively late discovery in Brazil (in the early 1700s), made a remarkable difference in the economic formation of the Spanish and Portuguese colonies. While the Spanish were taking tons of gold and silver to Europe, locals (administrative officials and natives) continued to rely on subsistence agriculture. Although their cultural treasures and metals were brutally stolen, the local populations were able to keep the traditional and collective agricultural know-how provided by traditional subsistence economies.

On the Portuguese side, the economy was mainly based on the economic cycles of large-scale monoculture farming (Furtado, 1991), such as the Brazil wood cycle, the sugar cane (and slave trade) cycle, the coffee cycle in the southeast, the rubber cycle in the Amazon and the livestock cycle in the northeast. The predominance of a large-scale monoculture economy had a huge impact on the formation of the new Brazilian social structure and culture, mainly because it deepened social inequality even further. The sugar cane plantation was designed to fulfill the need of another market (in this case Europe); it was based on unequal land and resource distribution; it did not require investment in labour education; and, worst of all, no matter how profitable these economic cycles were, the profits were never invested into the colony.

The local populations were socially and ecologically exploited by those driving the efficient and profitable large-scale economic cycles, which brought no returns to local society.

The African Influence

Yet another factor that distinguishes the Portuguese from the Spanish colonies in Latin America is the duration and intensity of the inflow of African men and women as forced immigrants. The nature of the slave trade and the slavery system, which served the demands of the large-scale economic cycles (especially on the sugar cane plantations), had an immense impact on Brazilian society and identity. This topic will be discussed in greater detail in *Chapter 4: A Case of Resilience*. Nonetheless, it is worth pointing out that the number of Africans brought to Brazil alone was larger than the number brought to all Spanish-speaking colonies together (including the French and British sugar colonies combined). The total number of Africans brought to Spanish Latin American countries during the whole slave period was roughly equivalent to US figures – and 10 times less than Brazilian figures (Tannenbaum, 1946).

In the Spanish colonies black Africans had come much earlier during the initial era of conquest and settling (Burkholder and Johnson, 2012). They were the descendants of African slaves imported into the Iberian Peninsula during the 15th century; by the time Columbus sailed, African slavery was well established in the peninsula (Burkholder and Johnson, 2012). Over a century later Africans in the Spanish side of Latin America were only about 13 percent of all slaves imported. These Africans were brought in smaller numbers to isolated mining regions in Honduras and Guatemala, and to the mining region of Potosí in Peru and Venezuela. In contrast, the slave trade in Brazil started later, in the second half of the 1500s, and lasted much longer (only in 1850 was the official slave trade in Brazil forbidden). There was also a constant inflow of new slaves in the following centuries, keeping their influence alive and stronger.

It is clear that all Latin American countries have tasted the bitter consequences of colonialism, though it is difficult to judge which colonization process was worse in socio-economic terms for its local people. (Of course, some elite groups in the region still believe the Iberians brought progress and civilization.) This chapter hopefully supports the idea that the different colonization processes between the Spanish and Portuguese territories of the continent can partly explain the differences in the economic, social and cultural formation of Latin American identities.

In this chapter I have chosen to focus on the historical and socio-economic development of the last five centuries on this side of the Atlantic in order to help us understand the patterns that created a distance between Brazilians and our neighbors. I acknowledge, however, the need to research further the cultural differences between the *colonizers*, namely Spain and Portugal. Their different characteristics must certainly have played a role in their approach to colonization and would no doubt shed further light on this discussion.

Discussing their perceptions about Brazil, a number of families from Mexico, Uruguay and Argentina have confirmed that they indeed experience a clear cultural difference (and distance) in their neighbors (or *hermanos*). They will often refer to the Brazilian informality as well as attitude towards authority, especially at work. They also tend to mention the quality of education and to the role of women; their perspective on the latter seems to be that Brazilians are 'too liberal'. As this chapter shows, the differences between the Portuguese and Spanish sides of South America are much more a consequence of the historical developments and differing colonial approaches in these territories than due to a language difference.

People from all Latin American countries would greatly benefit from closer collaboration, not only by coming to terms with our common past, but also by progressing and solving common challenges. It is up to each of us, on a national, academic and individual level, to focus on the similarities that sew together the pieces and to (re)create a more explicit, truthful and constructive Latin American pride.

Chapter 3
The Invisible Influence

Highlights

The current version of Brazilian history is questionable.

◆

Early encounters between the Portuguese and the indi-genous groups provide the framework for the Brazilian national identity.

◆

The definitions of 'developed' and 'primitive' people require revision.

◆

Many myths about the influence of the indigenous ethnic groups in the Brazilian culture make them invisible.

Chapter 3: The Invisible Influence

The early history of Brazilian colonization contains many examples of multiple *cultural shocks*, both *external shocks* between the different ethnic groups (Portuguese, Amerindians and Africans) and *internal shocks* in which individuals are constantly reevaluating who they are. As a mixed-blood Brazilian, rereading our *real* history caused me to reflect on my multi-ethnic identities, the dominant and non-dominant personalities who, in order to defend themselves, change roles between the aggressor and the victim, between killing and dying. I wonder if this isn't perhaps a typical internal struggle felt by many other Brazilians. It is certainly a way to make sense of the historical challenges we faced.

Reading about the first encounters of (my) two peoples from the opposite sides of the Atlantic (namely the *primitive* and the *civilized* versions of me) revived deep, inexplicable sensations under my 'creamy' skin. I realized how hard it is be impartial on such matters. It is difficult to talk about what happened during the three centuries of colonization without taking sides, without judging the 'good guy' versus the 'bad guy'… without wondering how things would have been had this encounter not happened. How would the native people of our continent, the Amerindians, and their holy environment be today if the Portuguese had not come? My curiosity to find out more about the nature of the early encounters and their impact on the formation of Brazil kept my motivation alive to move beyond my internal dilemmas.

History, and specifically the current version of it, should always be questioned. In any past event there are the facts and the characters – but there are also the observers, humans just like you and me, who tell the story based on their own perspectives and interpretations, and usually according to the context, values and ideologies of the time. History is often told (or not told) with a specific function or objective in mind and it can be used as 'truth' to convince, manipulate, and construct meanings. In this chapter, I will first explore the context in which the first intercultural contacts took place, and then the mentality and attitudes of the Portuguese at the time. Secondly, I will try to demystify the indigenous populations and debunk some common myths about them. I will also explain their contribution in the Brazil of today and why their influence became invisible in the last 500 years.

The common idea that Brazil was 'discovered' by the Portuguese about five centuries ago and that it became a colony dominated by this nation's customs, which were transplanted into the new continent, is a Eurocentric and limited view. The image of a great number of brave Portuguese conquering a few indigenous groups, who, together with their cultures, eventually disappeared, is nonsense. The scene of colonizers establishing 'real' civilization and saving the native pagan souls through the Christian faith usually completes this erroneous but popular picture of Brazilian history.

This version of Brazilian history is questionable for two key reasons. Firstly, because it was written by only one of the three central characters involved; namely the European invaders. What's more, the other two characters – the native indigenous peoples and the African slaves – could not read and write for the next couple of centuries. According to the writer and journalist Laurentino Gomes, in Brazil in 1822, the year of independence (322 years after the arrival of the Portuguese), only one in three people could read and write. We can only wonder how different it would be if Brazilian history had been written by the other two characters. Secondly, Brazil's history through the eyes of the other characters was purposefully made irrelevant for political, ideological and economic reasons; in the case of the indigenous population, a historical trick (or myth) made them invisible.

Unfortunately, if we want to learn about the Brazilian native population we should not ask the average Brazilian, as the general population knows little about it (and perhaps does not care) and almost nothing of this is taught in our schools. José R. B. Freire, Professor of Ethno-history at the University of Amazonas, Manaus, comments that knowledge about the indigenous cultural diversity is not taken seriously; research in Brazil is rather of 'Franciscan poverty' and reflects a deformed image of the indigenous peoples in our schools, media, and in Brazilian society (in Donisete & Grupioni, 1998). Where research in this area does exist, it is not successfully transmitted beyond academic circles to educational policies. As a result, transforming knowledge into action remains a challenge.

As in other parts of the world colonized by Europeans, the process of domination in Brazil took place through force and/ or manipulation justified by the materialistic values and ambitions of West European societies of that time and, in the case of Portugal, with the blessings of the Roman Catholic Church. To understand Brazil's history we cannot speak of a general *West European society*, because this does not describe the culture and mentality differences between, most strikingly, the north and south of Europe.

Colonization of Brazil was backed up by the ideologies of a hierarchical Portuguese society, which was in turn strongly influenced by the Catholic Church's counter-reform missions of 'salvation'. The Portuguese explorers brought with them highly developed navigation techniques as well as their experience at dominating other societies (during their earlier explorations in Africa), through both violent and non-violent methods. Unfortunately, the Portuguese also brought with them the old continent's history of wars for territorial dominance and power, and European ideas of what constituted superiority and civilization.

The European influence in Brazil presented mainly as a "Portuguese version of Europe" (Ribeiro, 2000). This differed in many aspects from the protestant northern countries, and had an impact on the Brazilian cultural formation and the kind of colony it became. Ribeiro differentiates between the northern and southern styles of colonization as the 'Gothic' and 'Baroque'. The North European peoples brought entire families to their colonies in the Americas, what is known as a *transplantation* of people. For them the native population was not a hindrance to their plans to settle. "Let them go and live where they want, free to be different but far away," was the general approach. Where the Iberian people colonized, mixing and miscegenation (or inter-breeding) with the native Amerindian population was common. Miscegenation occurred frequently mainly because the settlers were initially men only; families did not go to the new territory together (this will be discussed later in the chapter).

Compared to what happened in the Spanish colonies, and despite the European attitude towards human rights at the time, the domination (and to a certain extent, the acculturation) of the local ethnic groups took place in a rather non-confrontational manner in some regions of Brazil, even if this idea is controversial (Cunha, 2012). As we already know it took the European civilizations centuries (until the mid-1400s) to arrive at the illuminist ideas of social equality. Universal human rights, as we understand them today, were compromised by the existence of the nobility and limited by religious dogma. Humans were seen as inferior to God – an ideological construct – and they were further valued according to social class. Social, religious and ethnic discrimination are all part of European history; the Holocaust is just a recent example. Indeed, until as late as the 1500s, women in Europe were required to dress covering their bodies (and thus their sins) from head to toe. Furthermore, despite all manner of technological inventions by this stage, slavery was still an accepted practice.

Unfortunately, when the Iberians 'discovered' a distant new continent in the early 1500s, they brought this mentality with them. The Brazilian colony is no different to other colonies in this respect: the over-riding interaction between colonized and colonizer emphasized superiority/inferiority dynamics, as well as domination based on an inability to validate other peoples and cultures. European colonization methods reflected their intellectual and technological developments, as well as their advanced methods of domination. Progress, however, cannot always be defined in a straight and continuous line (Lévi-Strauss, 1952).

On meeting the indigenous population (the Amerindians), the Portuguese felt vastly superior in terms of intellectual and technological developments – the visible and concrete aspects of progress. They could show the native peoples their tools, weapons and possessions. Their superiority in this area was confirmed and so were their abilities to dominate, manipulate, explore and enslave the natives, for whom ideas of land ownership, materialistic ambition, social power and fear of burning in hell were new. This Portuguese attitude to subjugating others and establishing themselves in someone else's territory was imprinted in the history of the Brazilian identity from early intercultural interactions and has been present ever since.

Today we could claim that the human 'need' to feel superior reflects the lack of a wider idea of what development means. The word *development* has various meanings depending on the context and discipline. The concept of *development* in anthropology, for example, although fiercely debated, is generally connected to the concepts of *progress* and *modernity*. According to Schroder (1996), this definition has been used in different historical contexts and it should include political, economic and symbolic aspects at micro and macro levels. History seems to confirm that social beings can achieve a certain level of technological and intellectual development faster than moral development. In recent debates (Mahbub, 1996), sustainability, welfare, and feminist aspects are included in definition of development. Amartya Sen (1998 Nobel Prize winner in Economics), understands development "as freedom" in relation to "our ability to live as we would like" (Sen, 1997).

Psychologically speaking we can't talk about intercultural relations and different levels of development without talking about the cognitive biases of the mind. The idea that we are all worthy of the same amount of respect is not a visible and concrete concept; nor is it easily understood by all of human kind. It requires higher levels of abstract social skills and competencies for us to 'see' beyond the many superficial social and cultural layers and recognize what is essential, our common humanity.

Brazil is also not different from other colonies in which interactions between the colonizers and natives were based on social inequality and on economic domination by one (supposedly more developed) civilization over another. However, another way to expand our idea of

Chapter 3: The Invisible Influence

'development', which is usually judged according to technological/intellectual progress, emotional development by Daniel Goleman (1995) and moral aspects, is to include the concept of *ecological intelligence* – a concept used by Edson Gomes, a historian and archeologist whose contribution you will find in the last part of this chapter.

Based on his observations and visits to more than 200 ethnic groups, Gomes concludes that the native indigenous population can be considered highly ecologically developed. He believes the Amerindians have truly harmonious interactions with their environment, interactions which respect its time and its cycle allowing for natural rejuvenation. Although these interactions can be seen as entropic (which has a relative impact within time and space), they do not affect the macro-ecological structure of the land. On the contrary, this kind of approach enables a dynamic and perfect interaction between human and nature. In a study about the agriculture of the Kuikuru ethnic group, Carneiro (in Neves, 2000) suggests that the same area in Altos dos Xingu could be cultivated for up to 90 years.

The challenges of survival and the need to adapt and master one's habitat are usually the driving forces behind any human progress. The mental capacity and sensitivity to connect to one's physical environment – the ability to think long term and protect one's natural resources – is another example of higher-level abstract thinking. Should one talk in terms of *ecological development*, the Portuguese settlers would not emerge favorably. From the 1500s, 80 percent of the Brazilian coast (Mata Atlântica), once dense rain forest, was destroyed due to the Portuguese exploitation of Brazil wood and the repetitive monoculture plantations of sugar cane and coffee.

To understand the Brazil of today it is crucial also to delve deeper into the other characters in the country's history. With regards to the earliest indigenous peoples (the Amerindians), it is imperative that we understand:

1. Who they are;

2. Why their cultural influence on the general population was more intense and quite different when compared to the impact of indigenous cultures in North America;

3. Why their cultural influence was made invisible;

4. And finally, which elements of their culture are present in the Brazilian society of today.

The Amerindians are so called because they moved freely in the Latin American territory, which later became either Spanish or Portuguese. As a result some ethnic groups became separated – for example, the Guarani are in both territories today, but originally shared the same territory, language and costumes. They have adopted elements (including language) of their respective colonizers, but they were originally one ethnic group.

About 1,500 ethnic groups in the Brazilian territory have become extinct since 1500 (100 ethnic groups in the last century alone), although they did not all mysteriously 'disappear' as is commonly put forward in today's narrative of Brazil. It is almost impossible to know how many were incorporated into the new Brazilian society, as the criteria for 'white' or 'Indian' has never been clear. For example, an indigenous woman who married a white man was counted as white; social status defined racial classification and ethnicity.

We do know that 734,000 individuals, distributed in 230 ethnic groups with over 170 languages, survived extinction and exist in their specific ethnic groups in 582 indigenous reserves across Brazil (according to the Coordenação das Organizações Indígenas da Amazonia Brasileira, the Brazilian Coordination of the Indigenous Organization of the Amazon – COIAB). Of these about 50 remain isolated and have never been contacted by outsiders. Each ethnic group not only has a different language, which can be as different as Portuguese and German are to each other (Freire in Donisete & Grupioni, 1998), but also religion, art, science and history.

Huge numbers of indigenous groups who were enslaved lost their previous living conditions, habitats and identities over the centuries, while others were born into an underclass population of mixed-blood Brazilians. They too were incorporated into production activities as slaves – as late as 1655 – for there were no legal restrictions to keeping Amerindians in captivity until then. In truth, the demand for Indians slaves continued even beyond then. According to John Monteiro (in Donisete & Grupioni, 1998), in 1658 a priest by the name of Bettendorf registered 2000 Indians captured along the Amazon River alone.

Within their communities each member of the indigenous community has a different social function, although they usually have equal rights to express opinions and to be heard. Violence against women, children and the elderly rarely exist, as most interpersonal relations are known to be respectful. According to the anthropologist Pierre Clastres (1974), Western societies have an ethnocentric way of understanding primitive societies as they focus on what they think the other lacks: "They lack a State, they lack history, they lack literacy..." yet when it comes to leadership skills and decision-making processes, Western societies could learn a lot from indigenous Amerindian societies. The *cacique*, or leader, can be replaced whenever there is discontent; this is not a hereditary position. (Yet in many monarchic 'civilized' societies, changing leaders was not allowed.) Charisma and genuine leadership qualities are required for this role (qualities much like those demanded in today's business and government leaders). They have more than 'civilized' eyes can see.

But what happens if there is no power delegation or no appropriation of information? What if decisions are not taken by one person only? The result is that the relationship among group members becomes egalitarian, even between genders. For example, as noted by Orlando Villas Boas (in Neves, 2000), in the indigenous communities of the Xingu River no gender has power over the other. In these communities men and women may marry and separate as many times as they want, as there is no social sanction against this. Compare this to women in Western societies who were burning their bras and requesting equal rights only in the 1960s. Furthermore, on at least two occasions during the classic period of the Mayan civilization, women ruled city-states (Burkholder & Lyman, 2012). Just as the quality of interpersonal and gender relations in these indigenous societies is remarkable, so too is their adaptation to, and respect for, the environment. The land and its resources are communally owned and shared among people and other living beings. Humans are part of their universe, not its center.

The encounter between the Portuguese and the native Brazilian groups can be considered an encounter between a technologically advanced people, at their best in an expansionary mercantile period, and a people emerging from a 10,000-year-old Paleolithic state into the first stages of an agricultural revolution, living in pre-urban conglomerates (Ribeiro, 2000). Although, according to the anthropological points of view, the comparison between two groups as superior or inferior to each other has no scientific basis (Levi-Strauss, 1952). When it came to who dominated who, Portuguese technology, such as weapons, was decisive. However, the Amerindians had accumulated a vast knowledge of their environment. Knowledge such as where abundant resources could be found was essential for their survival in the tropics.

The native people depended for their food source on the generosity of tropical conditions, which were subject to seasonal changes marked by months of enormous abundance and months of scarcity (Ribeiro, 2000). It is widely accepted that without the guidance and know-how of the native people, the Portuguese would not have been able to expand and establish themselves inland. The importance of the indigenous people's knowledge of the tropical forest was again highlighted in the case of Henry Ford's attempt to produce rubber in the Amazon in the 1930s (Grandin, 2010). Despite enormous investments into technology and manpower, Ford's carefully established business plan neglected to take into account the challenges of surviving the rainy season, long distances, living conditions and threats to one's life (e.g. dangerous animals). He also ignored cultural differences, which made introducing the values of capitalism to the native people another unexpected barrier.

How then did the Portuguese manage to get their indigenous 'friends' to collaborate and work for them? As touched upon previously, the Portuguese understood the importance of being accepted into the fold; they understood that being perceived as an outsider would only create barriers to their interactions with the indigenous peoples. They also understood that the locals' concept of *work* was quite different to the Portuguese mentality, as was their source of motivation to work.

Intense Miscegenation

For almost 50 years in Brazil the only intercultural interaction was between the Amerindians and the Europeans (mainly Portuguese explorers, and some English and French illegal traders). Historical records reveal that all colonizers in this time were men, a fact highly relevant for our understanding of the formation of the contemporary Brazilian society and the intensity of the miscegenation that followed between these two groups (specifically, white Europeans and the indigenous women). Ribeiro (2000) calls it a cultural 'gestation' of the society. Early Portuguese settlements in Brazil were therefore different from those in the North American or Australian colonies; in the latter there was usually a transplantation of entire immigrant families, who, for many generations, tended not to blend with natives. The Portuguese, however, had found a rather different if disingenuous way of dominating the local people.

As we will see, the native Indians were not 'good' slaves and the violence, killings and threats used to subjugate African slaves proved ineffective. We have seen from their leadership structures, that the indigenous people were not accustomed to oppression. As a result the Portuguese had to come up with alternative strategies to make the indigenous people 'cooperate' and, in particular, help with finding Brazil wood. They realized that by mixing and having children with the Amerindian women they would be accepted and helped by the indigenous societies. This

Chapter 3: The Invisible Influence

approach is what historians today call *in-lawism* (or *cunhadismo*), a term created by Ribeiro (2000).

After seeing the extent of ethnic mixing between the colonizers and native peoples, the first governor, as well as the first missionaries arriving only in 1549, started a political campaign to bring Portuguese women to the colony. In their minds, what they saw would shock and embarrass European societies. In a letter dated 1550 and addressed to the Portuguese nobility ('Letters from Nobrega in 1955' in Ribeiro, 2000), the Jesuits called for Portuguese women of all classes to come to Brazil. "There are all classes of men here ... and in this way sin will be avoided and the population in the service of God will be increased," they wrote. Their call went largely unheeded. In 1551 three sisters of the Roman Catholic Church arrived; in 1553 came nine more and in 1559 another seven. According to Ribeiro these Portuguese women did not play much of a role in the making of the 'new' Brazilian family. Rather, for the first centuries of Portuguese colonization in Brazil, the Portuguese settlers bred with as many Amerindian women as they could. Ribeiro states: "By means of *cunhadismo* or 'in-lawism' carried to extremes, a 'new human breed' was created, which was not recognized or seen as such by Indians, by Europeans, or by blacks." According to the author this mixed population went on to make up the core of the nation in an ongoing process of acculturation, "a transition from the status of specific Indian with their attributes and customs, to the status of generic Indians".

In the indigenous societies, each individual functioned as an autonomous and independent member. Everyone in this society had to learn the survival skills to look after themselves and their families. When the indigenous populations were brought into the colonial society, they lost their autonomy and self-sufficiency; they became dependent. Furthermore, the indigenous people were sometimes brought by force to the urban areas and, being pagans (non Christians), were treated as 'incomplete humans' without souls. They could not speak their master's language and had no understanding of the cultural norms that were forced on them by the white people. They consequently lost their identity too.

As another consequence of intense miscegenation, the mixed-blood children born during the early centuries of colonization belonged neither to their culturally rich native families nor to the elite group of biological white fathers. Rather they blended into the rural and urban populations of Brazil as a lower class of people without land and, having the 'wrong' skin colour and faith, stood no possibility of being seen as equal and valuable members of the colony.

Understanding Why the Indigenous Influence is Ignored Today

The current version of Brazilian history, in which the Amerindian influence is rendered invisible, has been propagated due to four main (and erroneous) ideas:

1. Brazilian history, and consequently its culture, started about 500 years ago (from the Portuguese arrival in 1500);

2. The indigenous population was too small, primitive, nomadic and isolated to be considered important or relevant to the formation of the modern Brazilian culture;

3. Most of the indigenous population was killed, or died due to disease.

The first idea was easily proven wrong when archeological excavations in the Lagoa Santa area in the state of Minas Gerais found 'Luzia', the second oldest human skeleton ever found in the Americas (it is dated to around 11,500 to 12,500 years ago). In the Brazilian history textbooks this (very) long period is covered in only a couple of pages. Thus we do not learn that the indigenous peoples, whose societies lasted for thousands of years in South America before the arrival of the settlers, were remarkably developed, particularly in terms of social equality, individual autonomy, and ecological wisdom.

I have already touched briefly on the second idea – that there were only a few indigenous ethnic groups when the colonizers arrived, and that most of them 'disappeared' – but it deserves to be further demystified. When the Portuguese arrived in Brazil in 1500 the indigenous population was between five to seven million; in contrast, the population of Portugal at the time was one million. As Monteiro (in Donisete & Grupioni, 1998) points out, the Portuguese colonialists were a minority. Cunha (2012) states that, "if the indigenous people were many, there was not discovery but an invasion". During the early 1500s, the ratio of white Portuguese to Amerindian slave ranged from 1: 40 to 1:100. The total invasion of the immense Brazilian territory – as it was then – took place at a varying pace over the last five centuries. The indigenous population may have appeared to be an isolated group to the Portuguese because the latter had no idea of the size of the territory.

The third idea – that most of the indigenous individuals were all killed or died due to illnesses or diseases – cannot be more misleading. While

Chapter 3: The Invisible Influence

1500 ethnic groups became extinct, thousands of Amerindians were camouflaged by the poor, mixed-blood classes of Brazil, an issue not yet seriously explored. This is a social process, which even Brazilians remain unaware of – or perhaps they do not want to know. To be identified as being of Amerindian descent continues to be socially unacceptable in Brazil; it is a sign of belonging to the 'primitive' and underdeveloped parts of society. However, when we analyze many of the cultural behaviours of the majority of the 'semi-white' (or mixed blood) peoples in the Brazilian population we see great many similarities with the indigenous people. Historically, the terms mamelukes, caboclos or pardo were used interchangeably by the Brazilian Statistics Institution (IBGE, 2000) to name the undefined racial mixes (as I will explain in *Chapter 5: The Colonial Legacy Today*).

The fact is that the majority of the Brazilian population of today has Amerindian ancestry. This is more true for some regions than for others – perhaps depending on how long ago the indigenous ethnic groups were 'assimilated' into the new Brazilian society. Their influence is, without doubt, greater than originally believed. In genetic research carried out in 2007 by Sérgio Pena, Researcher at the Federal University of Minas Gerais, 60 percent of Brazilians who classified themselves as 'white' had Amerindian or African ancestry, particularly from their mother's side (Santos et. al., 2009).

In the beginning colonization focused on the quest for Brazil wood, the most valuable and highly appreciated natural resource on the European market at that time (gold had not yet been found). This activity was made possible mainly with the help of the indigenous population. Half a century later the focus turned to sugar and the accompanying African slave trade. The Portuguese Crown systematically enslaved the indigenous population too, as demand for labour increased in the sugar plantations. This process of removing indigenous people from their ethnic groups to serve as slaves was intense and prolonged (It continued for centuries in Brazil). There were many reports of deaths of the indigenous populations from diseases brought by the colonizers, but it is clear they did not all 'die out' or disappear. Rather, many were gradually assimilated into Brazilian society.

But when exactly does an individual stop being 'Amerindian' and become 'Brazilian'? How does he/she change from being a 'savage' to a 'civilized' member of society? When does the skin colour change from creamy to white? And finally, what changes in terms of social behaviour? Until 1824 when the first imperial constitution was introduced in Brazil, the slave population (Indian and African) was ignored; legally a slave was not considered a person, and consequently had no legal rights. In the case of the indigenous population individuals had to prove they had lived a minimum of five years as an integrated member of society to be considered legally capable, otherwise they were seen as having an 'incomplete maturity' or were considered orphans or mentally disabled (Filho in Donisete & Grupioni, 1998). This helps us understand why, in the Brazilian society of today, no one likes to be seen as being of Amerindian descent. Having general mixed blood, an undefined background, is considered better than being thought of as Indian.

Brazil – Not an Extension of Portugal

As well as the mistaken ideas about the influence of the Amerindians, it is common to hear that "Brazil is just an extension of Portugal". Yet we can find many reasons why the Brazilian culture isn't just a copy of the Portuguese culture. In colonization processes in other parts of the world, such as North America, Australia and New Zealand, there was a 'transplantation' of nuclear families who established themselves in the new continents and as immigrant communities. Though they did interact with natives, they did not mix with them as in Brazil. What happened in Brazil was a 'systematic new ethnic breeding' (Ribeiro, 2000). Even if the idea of Brazil as a copy-and-paste of Portugal is incomplete, it is still present in much training content about the Brazilian culture. Richard Lewis, in his book *When Cultures Collide*, mistakenly defines the Brazilian culture in this way:

> "Just as children inherit and imitate the behavioural characteristics of their parents, newborn states (usually colonies) inherit and adopt the cultural traits of the mother country. Brazilians – the only Portuguese-speaking people of Latin America – act quite differently from other South Americans because their mother country is Portugal, not Spain."

Yet how can the Brazilian culture be considered a child if the history of the Amerindians is over 11,000 years old? That is only possible if we accept the Eurocentric view that Brazil must be defined as a territory existing only after the Portuguese invasion five centuries ago. Yet, I believe, as happens with children, Brazilians inherited more from, and imitated more of, their Amerindian and African mothers than their unknown fathers. Unfortunately the mistakes continue. In most Brazilian history timelines, such as that on the BBC website (viewed on January 24th, 2012), the year 1500 is mentioned as the year of the 'discovery' of Brazil; the next important date is cited as 1808, when the Portuguese monarchy escaped Napoleon by moving to Brazil. And so three centuries of history is skipped, forgotten or ignored because no one likes to remember the ethnocide suffered by the Amerindians the extinction of 1500 different ethnic groups, not to mention the enslavement of Africans.

In terms of intercultural formation, the history of Brazil could instead be divided into three main phases:

1. The history of the Amerindians before 1500;

2. The history of the old settlers (the Amerindians, the Portuguese and their African slaves) and their integration, from 1500 until about 1850/ 1888;

3. The history of the recent immigrants (Italians, Germans, Polish, Japanese, and Lebanese, among others) who came to take the place of the 'freed' African slaves from 1888.

In the first phase we find thousands of ethnic groups living and interacting in the territory. In the second phase is an almost exclusively tricultural interaction among the Amerindians, Portuguese and Africans for almost four centuries (with some limited interaction with French and Dutch traders). In the third phase we find the arrival of all other recent immigrants, which took place intensively only in the 20th century. Having acknowledged these three broad phases, it is clear that the influence of the later immigrants on the identity of Brazil is relatively recent and highly overvalued. When these immigrants arrived the core foundation of the modern Brazil was already formed. This may explain why these immigrants had (and still have) difficulties in adapting to the (already established) culture.

Immigrants from many nationalities have had problems integrating into the Brazilian culture they arrived in. Historical documentation reveals that the first (more recent) European, Japanese and even Chinese immigrants who came following colonial propaganda were shocked by the living and working conditions, for the colony was used to treating workers as slaves. The Chinese government prohibited their nationals from immigrating to Brazil after a disastrous attempt between 1812 and 1819 to bring 300 immigrants in to cultivate tea in the state of Rio de Janeiro. The main complaint was how poorly they were treated (Shang Sheng, 2009). The elite white slave-owners of the time had become used to treating their slaves (and thus their workers) how they pleased.

To properly understand the Brazil of today, we must acknowledge the power of the earlier tricultural interaction and its important role in modern

Brazilian culture. Brazilian scholars have debated the relevance of 'the myth of the three races', an idea first proposed not by a Brazilian, but by a German naturalist called Karl Von Martius (Schwarcz, 1993). The Portuguese Crown refused to accept this uncomfortable tri-racial version of history; instead they sustained the view of Brazil as an extension of Portugal with other European influences. It was uncomfortable because the Portuguese did not want to consider the importance of the Indigenous and African influence in the Brazilian formation. The interaction with the recent immigrants is important too, mainly because it is recent, more visible, and easily identified; yet we must not overestimate its role in the intercultural formation of Brazil. The Brazilian perception of its own culture has always reflected an external, imaginary figure, an ideal of national identity that dictates we must be whiter and more European than we really are. This ideal national figure forces us to be ashamed of our mixed, coloured faces. Ribeiro (2000) describes this search for identity as an external pressure, and advocates "a process to discover who we are and not who it would suit them for us to be".

It is obviously difficult (and perhaps of no value) to ascertain who has had more influence in the Brazilian culture of today; however, the need to include the influence of the indigenous cultures is self-evident. Historically there has always been a dualistic view of the Amerindians (they were seen either as evil, primitive creatures capable of cannibalism or in the naïve idyllic model; the good or the bad, but little in between). Yet it is clear this view is highly simplistic, not to mention unjust. Furthermore, their characteristics remain and should be properly addressed by anyone who is serious about understanding our culture. This analysis becomes relevant especially when it comes to how the Brazilian people deny it and how they choose to interpret it in order to create an individual and national identity.

Insights from an expert

In my search for more insight into the diverse cultures of the indigenous population, I was fortunate to meet Edson Gomes, a historian, archeologist, and founder of the private museum of Indian art, Ameríndia Arte Indígena in Campinas, São Paulo. After being based in the Amazon, close to an indigenous territory, Edson left his military career to study the Amerindians. Today, he owns an indigenous art collection and his archeological museum is visited mostly by foreigners, many of whom work in museums around the world. Edson confirms that, in general, Brazilians do not appreciate the diversity and richness of the art and history of today's indigenous populations; for most Brazilians, he says, this is just folklore.

With his help, I wanted to clarify some of the myths about the indigenous peoples. In our first conversations, Edson gave me a disapproving look every time I used the word 'Indians'. He explained that 'Indian' is too generic a term to convey the uniqueness of language, culture and diversity of the Amerindian population. The term was first used by the Iberian invaders, who mistakenly believed they had arrived in India. Edson has worked with and visited over 200 indigenous ethnic groups who, according to him, would be offended to be called 'Indians'; rather, they should be referred to as the Bororó, the Tupinambá, the Yanomani, the Kayapó, etc.

In his impressive shop (called Ameríndia), surrounded by his rare collections of indigenous art, adornments, weapons, ceramics, lace and fabrics, musical instruments, ritual objects, weaving tools and wooden utensils, our conversations would last hours. We shared our embarrassment and disappointment that most Brazilians do not understand, appreciate or respect the indigenous cultures – even if we incorporate many of their values and characteristics, such as our attitudes to time, rebellious spirits, and generosity) as part of our social values (more on this in Chapter 5: The Colonial Legacy Today). We lamented the activities of international mining companies, whose commercial interests in the indigenous territories have become the biggest threat to their protection. These commercial activities also threaten the survival of the many resident ethnic groups, respectable members of our society who, we believe, have so much to teach us.

Edson strongly believes the indigenous population would live much as they did before the Portuguese came, if they had the choice, as they had no reason or environmental challenges to force a change. When I asked him why the Amerindians in Brazil had never built any great constructions (such as pyramids, or impressive cities) and what their contribution to the history of civilization was, Edson's reply was swift and proud: their most valuable contribution was that they preserved the environment and kept it almost entirely intact. Without their protection the ecological destruction could have been much worse.

Many of the cultural elements of the indigenous population exist as part of the Brazilian society of today, making the Brazilian culture a complex one. Those remaining ethnic groups who still live in their communities, only about one percent of the population (817,963 people according to IBGE, 2010), play a vital role in the solution; they teach us about harmonious social interactions and the preservation of the environment for future generations. The value of these people, who have survived three centuries of brutal colonization and another two centuries of national neglect, must be affirmed within our national identity. Their influence in the Brazilian culture is stronger than ever, especially with the rise of the poor classes (referred to as the D, E and F social classes in market research and official statistics). Their influence continues to be invisible to those whose ears and eyes remain unable to accept the uniqueness, wisdom, and endurance of these peoples.

Chapter 4
A Case of Resilience

Highlights

The implications of slavery, conditioned slavery, and post-slavery systems in the Brazilian culture continue to be underestimated.

◆

A comparison between the US and Iberian slavery systems reveals some root causes of the Brazilian socio economic reality.

◆

The legacy of the dualistic colonial society – 'slave and his master' – reinforces the ambiguity of the Brazilian identity.

◆

The debate about official apologies over slavery: a forgotten history or an unresolved past?

Chapter 4: A Case of Resilience

Often I wonder how interculturalists (or anyone for that matter) can discuss the Brazilian culture without seriously approaching the themes of slavery, conditioned slavery, and post slavery. Most intercultural trainings about Brazil neither mention these nor explore their implications. Maybe this reflects a desire, as human beings, to deny the horrendous but real parts of our past – or maybe the link between slavery and some cultural aspects of Brazilians of today remains unclear. For some, rationalizing that slavery existed in many other civilizations is enough to lessen their guilt or powerlessness when confronting such a base act.

I once met a Portuguese couple who had recently moved to Brazil and the topic of slavery came up in our conversation. At one point the woman remarked, "In Portugal, nowadays, people really are not aware of what we did here in Brazil during the colonial time, they do not know what happened, they do not talk about it, period!" Few people want to know about some frankly unforgettable facts. In 1500 there were about 25,000 slaves in the Old World, while in Africa captives of war existed but no slave trade – until the arrival of the Europeans (Mattoso, 1996). Slavery flourished in the Iberian Peninsula especially following the continuing wars with the Moors and the early contact with Africa. In Andalusia there were not only black slaves, but also Moorish, Jewish and Spanish slaves in the 1400s (Rinchon in Tannenbaum, 1946).

Although slavery existed before, it was the *intensity* of the trade to the New World, and the demand for labour in the sugar cane plantations, that created the association between a slave and a black person. Some historians have argued that the profits from trade and slave-based agriculture in the Americas played a central role in financing modern capitalism (Burkholder & Johnson, 2012).

Even in Sweden, a highly politically correct country and where I currently live, it is surprising to find that the average person does not know slavery was practiced in the West Indian island of Saint-Barthélemy (commonly known as St. Barts) while administered by the Swedish Crown. (In 1771, when Gustav III became King of Sweden he wanted to re-establish the country as a European 'great power' and acquired the island from France.) Slavery was practiced under the "Ordinance concerning the policing of slaves and free coloured people" of 1787 (Skytte, 1986).

Indeed, the island was operated as a *porto franco* (free port). Although it was considered relatively insignificant as an island – it had no strategic position being very poor and dry – it became a successful business for Gustav. As owner of 10 percent of the Svenska Västindiska Kompaniet (Swedish West India Company), which was granted the right to trade slaves between Africa and the West Indies, he received one quarter of all profits. The (Swedish) Saint-Barthélemy government charged a small export duty on slaves sold from Saint Barthélemy to other colonies. This duty was halved for slaves imported from Africa on Swedish ships, generating increased profits for the West India Company and other Swedish traders. In March 1790 a new custom tax and constitution were introduced to the island. Both were designed to make Saint-Barthélemy a haven for slave traders. The new laws gave astonishing opportunities for traders from all over the world to buy and sell slaves tax-free. The last legally owned slaves in the Swedish colony were granted their freedom by the state in October 1847.

Conveniently 'forgetting' the past seems to be a human trait, even in Brazil, where slavery was a 'normal' part of society for (officially) 338 years. Yet more than three centuries of slavery inevitably had a profound impact on the cultural dynamics and the quality of social interactions. According to this classical historian:

> "... whenever we had slavery, we had a slave society, not merely for the blacks, but for the whites, not merely for the law, but for the family, not merely for the labor system, but for the culture – the total culture. Nothing escaped, nothing was beyond or above or outside the slave institution; the institution was the society in all its manifestations." (Tannenbaum, 1946)

Slavery, in general, imprinted a peculiar relationship between the ruler and the ruled, the superior and the inferior, the rich and the poor, leaving very little outside of this relationship. This theme is much explored by the Brazilian anthropologist Gilberto Freyre in *The Masters and the Slave* (1964). Other authors, including Katia Mattoso, a French historian who lived in Brazil, acknowledge the importance of all other social interactions of the time, especially those between the slave born in Africa, the slave born in Brazil; the manumitted slave (who was given freedom as a gesture of 'gratitude' for being a 'devoted servant' after long years of service); the conditioned manumitted slave (who was given freedom after fulfilling certain conditions, such as making a payment or working for free for a set time); the freed slave (in general) and the free man. (More details about the implications of these interactions will be covered in *Chapter 5: The Colonial Legacy Today*.)

Reading and writing about slavery and its unspoken details has not been an easy task for me. I still remember the day my best playmate – who was black – was 'adopted' by my grandmother at around the age of 12. She had to work as a servant in exchange for food, shelter and schooling. At that time I did not yet understand that such an ambiguous arrangement was a legacy of our past. My research into slavery reminds me of my own difficulties in coming to terms with this hurtful part of our history. I cannot see another way to ease this pain other than to confront it, to examine the wounds and then to take care of them. Hopefully they will heal one day. In a typical Brazilian family it is not hard to identify a 'darker' grandmother or grandfather. Yet we learn early to focus on the 'whiter' side of the family, and to straighten our curly hair (also called 'cabelo ruim', the 'bad hair') so we can better fit into society.

From the Brazilian perspective there are innumerable tones between white and black, which enable us to define ourselves as 'morenos', which means 'not white', but especially 'not black'. Only in very recent years have there been positive changes in the way the Brazilian society sees, and incorporates, black people; there is still a long way to go. We hear mostly about the African influence in our food, music, religion and folklore. We do not hear often enough about how Africans really contributed to our society, or about how former slaves were thrown into society in the post-slavery period, and the problems that followed.

The first objective of this chapter is therefore to further acknowledge and highlight the existence of slavery (intensively and extensively throughout the Brazilian territory). The second is to explore the differences between slavery in the US and Brazil, for this can help us to then understand the particularities of the Iberian slave system. The third objective is to identify the implications of certain historical events for the Brazilian society of today, such as the impact on the Brazilian family structure and the essence of the often-dualistic social dynamic. By taking a closer look at seldom spoken historical facts, as I do throughout this book, my intention is to help us to see beyond generalizations.

The Reality of Slavery in Brazil

Brazil imported 38 percent of all slaves brought to the New World (approximately 3.6 million people), until 1850 when the slave trade was officially forbidden. Between 1502 and 1860 more than 9,500,000 Africans were brought to the Americas (there is no consensus among historians as to the exact number). It is worth repeating that until the abolition of slavery in 1888 Brazil received approximately 10 times the number of African slaves than the United States; the latter received about the equivalent number of slaves as all other Latin America countries combined. Brazil has the largest population of Africans outside the African continent.

Here too we make the rather basic mistake of using the generic term 'Africans'. According to Reginaldo Prandi (2000), the Africans who were brought to Brazil originated, in general, from two main linguistic groups, the Sudanese and the Bantu, as well as some minor Islamic groups. Both the Sudanese and Bantu constituted various other linguistic and ethnic subgroups. For example, the Sudanese came from both the north (Nubians, Baric) and the central African Nagoya (or Yoruba). The Yoruba consisted of numerous subgroups based on differences in language and culture, such as the Oyo, Ijexá, Ketu, Ijebu, Egbá, Ifé and Oxogbô. Within the Bantu group between 700 and 2000 dialects were spoken. This rich linguistic diversity of Africans was unfortunately almost completely lost in the Americas.

As discussed earlier the human mind has a tendency to generalize and put whatever is unfamiliar into one generic category (e.g. the Africans). Unfortunately, most of us (Brazilian and non-Brazilian) continue to be unaware of this great diversity of the African continent, both because our history books do not teach it and because the 'elite' (the dominant white minority) sees no reason to expose events they want to forget.

At this point it is important to emphasize not only the intensity of slave trading, but also its extent. There is a general perception (among Brazilians too) that slaves were in specific regions only, such as Bahia. Slavery was, in fact, spread across all regions of Brazil, even in the 'whiter' southern region. In 1819 the percentage of slaves in the population varied between regions from 27.3 to 40.7 percent (see Table 1). In the south – where a few centuries later (in the early 1900s), immigrants such as Germans and Italian arrived – 28.9 percent of the population were slaves. In 1889, in Pelotas, a city in the southern state of Rio Grande do Sul, 9000 of the total population of 20,000 were slaves (Gomes, 1989).

Region	Percentage of slave population	
	in 1819	in 1872
North	27.3	8.5
Northeast	33.0	9.4
East	28.1	19.5
South	28.9	16.0
Center west	40.7	7.8
Total	**30.0**	**15.0**

Table 1. Brazilian Slave Population compared to Total Population (Skidmore, 1974)

Chapter 4: A Case of Resilience

More recently, in 2010, 51 percent of the population classified themselves as black or '*pardo*' (semi-black), according to the Strategic Brazilian Organization, or SAE (Secretaria de Assuntos Estratégicos). This shows an increase in recent decades, likely due to a slightly better level of social acceptance as well as recent government social benefits including employment opportunities and places reserved for African descendants at public universities. However, self-classified skin colour has (unfortunately) always been considered more relevant to government policy-making than actual ancestry; as we will discuss later in this chapter, the self-classification methods used to count the population in Brazil soon became an official fiasco.

Slavery was a part of colonial life not only in the rural areas (such as the sugar cane plantations and gold mining areas), but also in the urban areas. A visitor to Bahia in the early 16th century noted that even in urban areas "there is not a single Portuguese, however poor, man or woman, who does not possess two or three slaves who earn their master's living" (Mattoso, 1996). Yet, perhaps as an attempt to minimize the centuries of slavery, even Brazil's legislators completely ignored the centuries of slavery in the first constitution in 1824 – they chose not to acknowledge slavery at all, ignoring the existence of the whole institution, slaves' rights, and the possibility of compensation. As discussed earlier 'forgetting' that part of history was yet another ideological and political trick played by those who wrote our history. As a 'prize', the ruling elite and our society could 'win' the world record of being the last country to abolish slavery, in 1888.

Ethnicity has always been an important element of the national identity because it describes not only a person's skin colour but also their background, and thus their place in society. This is not a topic spoken about explicitly; rather it is avoided, if not distorted. Miscegenation and racial classification in Brazil are two controversial themes that make the 'official' Brazilian history something of a joke. The Brazilian Institute of Geography and Statistics (IBGE), which has conducted censuses in Brazil since 1940, acknowledges the biases in counting and classifying races that have characterized Brazilian population data collection (Araújo, 1987). The 1872 and 1890 population censuses by the IBGE counted '*caboclos*' (White-Amerindian mixed race individuals) as a distinct category; in the 1890 census, the category '*pardo*' (semi-black) was replaced with '*mestiço*' (person of any mixed racial ancestry); the 1900, 1920 and 1970 censuses did not count people according to 'race' at all. In the 1940 census people were asked for their colour or race; if the answer was not 'white', 'black', or 'yellow', interviewers were instructed to fill the box with a slash. These slashes were later described in the category '*pardo*'.

In practice this means answers such as 'pardo', 'moreno', 'mulato' and 'caboclo' were counted as one category. Yet, if allowed to choose their classification, Brazilians will give almost 200 different answers (Schwartzmann, 1999). In another survey, in an attempt to simplify the terms Brazilians use to classify themselves, researchers narrowed them down to 136 categories, then into 28 broader categories. Most of these categories can be situated in the white-black continuum of answers to the open-ended question, "what is your race?" (Petrucelli, 2007). In summary, the biases found in race classification show that Brazilians want to be classified as whiter than we genetically are; the results of the race self-classification reflected this deep wish.

Ethnicity is an important aspect of the Brazilian identity even if the intense miscegenation made it blurred. As mentioned earlier, it only takes our brains within one to two tenths of a second to start categorizing race. What we call 'identity' is an abstract and dynamic concept. In reality it is a process through which people (individually and collectively) negotiate and construct meaning. In this process to construct the idea of who we are, Brazilians tend to deny the responsibility of looking back to our slavery history and facing the facts – and especially the social consequences. Many sectors of the Brazilian society, except the slaves and their descendants, continue to deny that we profited economically from this system and its brutal means of human subjugation. Slavery was not invented in Brazil, but the Brazilian society let it happen and took advantage of it, directly or indirectly.

At that time in Europe, external, visible reflections of difference, such as appearance (e.g. skin colour) or unfamiliar behaviours, were seen to justify inequality and the discounting of basic human rights of those 'others'. Violence and cruelty to other (non-white) races and cultures was thus considered normal. The ideology in Europe at that time was based on *mercantilism*, a dominant school of thought throughout the late Renaissance and early modern period (from the 15th to the 18th century). Mercantilism encouraged the many intra-European wars and fueled European expansion and imperialism (Popkin, 1966). The word *Eurocentrism* has its origin in colonialism. It was based on the values of the mediaeval intellectual world of Western Europe, which put Europe at the center of the world. This perspective of the world was later challenged somewhat by, among other things, waves of discoveries and voyages of exploration from Portugal and Spain. However, "these mediaeval views [of Europe as central] continued to be expressed in various forms well into the seventeenth century" (Popkin, 1966).

The Portuguese colonizers, blinkered by this ideology, did not appear to be seeing the intrinsic qualities common to all of humanity. Even though they were a minority (or perhaps because of it), they wanted to defend their identity as a white European transplanted society through all available means. In vain, according to Matoso (1996), for "one found few European-born women, and sexual needs could not be denied". The same dominant elite still struggle today to acknowledge that skin colour continues to decide the destinies of millions of African descendants in Brazil. How much longer can we ignore what really happened? This was one of the greatest population movements of all time and its effects cannot be swept under the carpet.

The lessons to be learned from centuries of slavery depend on how we incorporate this part of history – and its socio-cultural and economic consequences – within our conscious minds. Unfortunately ambivalence, one of the characteristics and consequences of colonialism, remains strong in our society (often I wonder if 'hypocrisy' wouldn't be a more appropriate description). In 1995 Brazilian regional newspaper, *Folha de São Paulo*, ran a poll asking Brazilians if racism existed; over 80 percent answered "yes". But, when asked, "Have you ever discriminated against someone?" the majority answered "no". This led anthropologist and writer Kabengele Munanga (2012) to wonder: "can racism exist without racists?" From an intercultural point of view this kind of ambivalence reveals who we are and who we want to be. When attitudes like this prevail it deepens our understanding of how history and social dynamics can impact cultural formation. (We will further explore the ways ambivalence shapes behaviour in *Chapter 6: Leadership Skills in Brazil*.)

The Individuals

Historians estimate that about one third of Africans taken from their home countries died on the way to the African coast and at embarkation stations, another third died crossing the ocean, while the final third became the forced immigrants, or slaves. Across the centuries, in an attempt to avoid acts of rebellion, Africans arriving in Brazil were carefully divided by the Portuguese into mixed groups; that is, with those from different ethnic origins, speaking other languages. Unable to understand each other, this prevented them from becoming organized and resisting as a group until they had learned Portuguese. Most authors and historians agree that, no matter how hard we try, we will probably never fully understand what these men, women and children suffered, nor can we fully grasp the impact this had on generations to follow.

We can, however, admire their innate capacities and learned abilities to survive despite (and as a result of) this suffering.

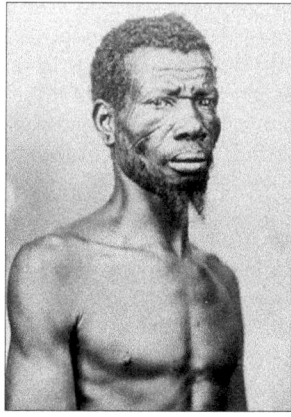

The marks on the face of the man above are believed to be self-inflicted and done in order to identify his ethnic origins. Photo by August Stahl, circa 1800s

Resilience (defined by the *Oxford English Dictionary* as '*a capability to recover, strength, elasticity, adaptability, toughness*') was key to the survival of those who were sold into slavery and into one of the most profitable economic activities ever (for some). They crossed the Atlantic (a 35-50 day trip in the overcrowded hold of the ship) into enforced labour so that people on the Old Continent could enjoy the sweet taste of sugar and decorate their churches in gold – while the slave traders became rich and powerful in Brazil, Europe and Africa.

Despite what some people might believe, "where there is slavery there is resistance" (Grinberg, 2001). In the previous chapter I mentioned that the Amerindians were not considered 'good slaves' because of their insubordination. African slaves also resisted albeit in a different manner. Even among those African slaves who did not try to escape, there was a silent resistance throughout the three long centuries. In 1813 Liberata, a slave, systematically sexually abused from the age of 10 and given the promise by her owner, José Rebello, that she would one day be freed, went to the courts and, after many years, got her freedom. There were 400 such cases from the 19th century onwards, recently studied by Grinberg, (2001). In most of these cases the slave, after many years saving money, had tried to buy their freedom but were denied this by their owners, who either raised the price or took their money. As slave children cost less, mothers often bought *their* freedom before buying their own.

Obedience and compliance were expected from all slaves at all times. Swallowing one's pride and doing as you were told was one way to (temporarily) guarantee food and protection. On a personal level the slaves had to resign to the paradox that they did not own their own bodies, but 'their souls were free' – as explained by the Catholic Church (who nonetheless considered them God's children). Collectively their individuality and richness were expressed mainly through religious rituals, music and dance. The African voice within lost its origins and identity, but not its wisdom and endurance. The Brazilian national identity remains incomplete until we 'meet', with joy and respect, this part of us. I believe we should ask ourselves explicitly: "What has our society learned from Africans and the slavery experience?" and "Which African virtues and attitudes enrich us as Brazilians?"

Slavery in the US and in Brazil

In 2011 I met an African American family who had relocated temporarily to Brazil for the wife's work. The family, who are well educated, moved with their teenagers to a relatively well-off region of São Paulo State. They soon realized their teenagers were the first black children to attend (and graduate from) the private international school they had chosen. (In general, Brazilians are not used to meeting well-educated black people – in Brazil they remain the exception to the rule.) Their experiences as a black family in Brazil came as a shock to them. For example, the husband was stopped by the local police a few times while walking along the street, because he 'looked suspicious'; they let him go when they realized he was American and spoke English. This kind of discrimination continued throughout the family's stay in Brazil. (Kabengele Munanga, an anthropologist from Congo who lives in Brazil, has had similar experiences.)

After hearing how this family was treated, I was motivated to investigate the differences between the United States and Brazil and how these differences might help us understand the impact of a history of slavery on cultural behaviour. One would imagine that discrimination is discrimination everywhere we go, but it does not work like that. There are remarkably different nuances between the two countries.

The first (and obvious) difference is the ethnic definition of 'black' and 'afro descendant'. In the US 'African American' is a clear definition or classification, as there was little miscegenation between black and white people in the US's slavery story. From the American standpoint, and in line with genetic research, almost all Brazilians would be considered of Black or Amerindian descent (proportions of African and Amerindian genetic markers vary along with the European ones). In the Brazilian Portuguese language, however, the term 'African Brazilian' was rarely used. The 'indisputable' blacks are most of the time associated with poverty, lack of education, and criminality – a general idea shared by many, even if often unconsciously. Only recently, as a result of movements to validate their heritage, has the term '*afrodescendentes*' at last found its way into Brazilian society, and been used by academics, politicians, media and the people themselves.

As well as the different racial/ cultural definitions (and connotations associated with them), the classic comparative study of race relations in the Americas by Frank Tannenbaum (*Slave and Citizen*, 1946) can help us clarify the ideological, legal and educational differences of the slavery systems in the southern states in the US and in Brazil.

Ideological and Legal Differences

In the Iberian Peninsula, as discussed earlier, people were no strangers to slavery. The persistence of a long tradition of slave law according to the Justinian Code influenced the belief, paradoxically, in the equality of men under the law (Tannenbaum, 1946). Justinian code was the legal code of ancient Rome, set out by Justinian, under which a magistrate could award a thing or a person to another person, essentially from debtor to creditor, and in turn a justification for slavery. The Brazilian slave system inherited this tradition, which in turn was framed by the Catholic doctrine. Thus, in Brazil, the prevailing ideology – supported by the Church – was of *spiritual equality* between the slave and his master; slavery was therefore considered an unfortunate condition. In other words there was still a concept of the individual's value as a human being, implying a circumstantial and gradual possibility of freedom (often in exchange for economic compensation). Specifically, slavery was seen as a product of 'accident and misfortune' (Tannenbaum, 1946). It was believed that slavery affects only the body, which may belong to the master, but that the soul of the slave remained free.

In the US slaves were not perceived as having any human value and were considered incapable of achieving freedom; abolition in this case had to be achieved by force (revolution) and could only be

Chapter 4: A Case of Resilience

guaranteed by law. The colour of the skin was believed to determine their condition: slaves, and forever.

Consequently there were legal differences between the two systems of slavery. In Brazil, freedom was a matter of financial compensation: the slaves were manipulated to believe that, if they behaved appropriately, there was the possibility (a farce, in many cases) to buy their own freedom even if this could take many years. There were always many conditions and possibilities to pay by installments. These agreements were referred to as *conditioned slavery* or *conditioned freedom (manumission)*.

In the US, manumission (the possibility to be given or buy freedom) was prohibited, with the rare exception. In South Carolina, Georgia, Alabama and Mississippi manumission was valid only with the consent of the state legislature. A fine was usually imposed and the freed slave had to leave the state within 90 days, never to return. Slaves were looked upon as a morally and biologically inferior. For the first time in history the association between the black colour and slavery was presumed. Mississippi prohibited a master from allowing his slave to trade like a free man, as well as the ownership of animals by slaves (Tannenbaum, 1946).

In Brazil, although the slavery abolitionist movement existed, there were less intense large revolts (which lead nowhere) through the 16th to 18th centuries. Running away into the expansive interior presented a more attractive alternative than the dangers of revolt (Bergad, 2007). Abolition, therefore, was not a result of war, but rather a political decision resulting from national and international pressure (mainly from Britain). It was nonetheless a slow process; the importation of slaves from Africa continued and even increased after the official slave trade prohibition of 1850.

In the US the prohibition of slave trade took place in 1808 (42 years earlier than in Brazil) and the abolition of slavery in 1863, with Lincoln's final Emancipation Proclamation – the result of a violent civil war. After abolition, and despite white resistance, blacks were guaranteed minimum rights that included owning land and attending school. The change in the ideology (or the beginning of the change) was anchored by the law. Laws and regulations are generally respected in the US, as they are usually the result of a long democratic process. This had implications for post-slavery social support. For example, the South Homestead Act of 1866 guaranteed the right of freed slaves to be the primary beneficiaries of 46 million acres of public land for sale in 160-acre plots in the southern states of Alabama, Arkansas, Florida, Louisiana and Mississippi (Williams, 2000).

Educational Differences

The differences in the two post-slavery societies are striking, particularly with respect to education and government assistance. Schooling of slaves was strictly prohibited in Brazil (Mattoso, 1996) until abolition in 1888. My generation witnessed this lack of even basic social support from the Brazilian government, which created many generations of illiterate 'freed' people. Black children in Brazil did not have schools to go to; due to extreme poverty they did not have access to the public schools and children instead worked to help support the family. Educational policy simply didn't account for their inclusion. Only in the 1990s did the government create financial incentives for poor families to keep children in school; until then, poor black children were still begging at traffic lights.

In contrast, during the civil war period in the United States, there was a huge push for black children to be allowed to go to the same schools as white children. Numerous private academies and colleges for freed men were established by northern missionaries. Each state created colleges for the newly freed men, such as Alcorn State University in Mississippi. As early as 1890 black state colleges started receiving federal funds as land grant schools (institutions that have been designated by its state legislature or Congress to receive the benefits of the Morrill Acts of 1862 and 1890). They continued to receive state funds even after the 'reconstruction' period of the civil rights movement, due to the influence of powerful liberals (even in the southern states) who were strongly in favor of having the state provide education for all races.

The dearth of post-slavery support for the freed people in Brazil inevitably had long-lasting consequences. Afro descendants in Brazil not only carry the burden of being associated with slavery, but also the socio-economic consequence of being abandoned by the Brazilian ruling elite even after slavery had ended. In 1822, the year of our independence, two out of three Brazilians could not read or write (Gomes, 2010). Such was the extent of marginalization and discrimination that, when I was growing up, if we saw a black person driving a car, we automatically assumed, "he's the driver" or even worse, "has he stolen it?"

Most American historians consider the efforts in the 'reconstruction' period to be insufficient. These were nonetheless substantially more than the efforts made in Brazil. In Brazil, there was no such a thing as a reconstruction period after abolition. There was instead negligence; no initiatives were launched to compensate for centuries of slavery. Even after abolition took place the economy was still fully dependent

Chapter 4: A Case of Resilience

on 'cost free' labour. This negligence by the government to support the freed slaves is, in my opinion, one of the most serious mistakes we have ever made. The consequences of this post-slavery period can be seen everywhere in the Brazil of today. As well as the lack of support for policies such as minimum living conditions, the ideology continues that it is okay not to spend public money on taking care of people. It is as if the majority of the population, the poorest of our society, did not count; they did not exist.

Only very recently, during the latest financial crisis, has the importance of social classes D, E and F (the legacy of the past) come into the spotlight – and for economic reasons only – as a potential purchasing power. The latest global economic retraction, whereby most of our export markets (developed world markets) decreased expenditure on Brazilian goods, showed the importance of having an internal market. Suddenly our government (and citizens in general) realized that this two-thirds of the population make a difference; at least, an economic difference. Making sure the mass population eats and purchases goods became part of the economic strategy.

Many Brazilians, especially from the dominant elite, still question the need for inclusive social policies. Hopefully, by becoming economically important, the mass population will become important as individuals, as people worth investing in, independent of their colour and background. In this way, I hope we will change our ideology. Unfortunately there does not seem to be a shortcut to creating a more just society – providing basic needs and rights is not luxury, but rather a long-term investment.

The difference in duration of the slave trades in the US and in Brazil also led to differences in their respective socio-economic systems. All of the Southern colonies, except Georgia, had banned or limited the African slave trade by 1786; Georgia did so in 1798 (Trinkley, 2007). As trade was forbidden, slave owners could not replace them. The only alternative was to support slave family ties so that children would become the master's new labour force. Ironically, this had some positive effect on family structures and the way slaves were consequently treated. In Brazil the slave trade (importation from Africa) was only forbidden in 1850, but (as we saw earlier) illegal traffic maintained the inflow of slaves for much longer, probably up until the official abolition of slavery in 1888. This had a direct negative effect on how slaves were taken care of and especially on the need to support family ties and structures. The Iberian slave owners were consequently able to maintain their 'short-term' brutal attitude to labour as they faced no shortage of slave supplies. In the US, after slave trade prohibition, the law was reinforced. As a consequence prices went up and slave owners had to take better care of their slaves as they could not easily replace them.

At face value the Brazilian slavery system may appear less hostile than the American system, as it allowed freedom to be bought. On the other hand educational and socio-economic negligence following the banning of slavery deepened discrimination and restricted any upward social mobility. The differences discussed thus far also highlight the important role of the legal system (which enforces educational and socio-economic policies) to implement social change. The strict American legal system was capable of enforcing civil rights even in an ideologically antagonistic environment, while the Brazilian legal system, which remained biased, weak and ambiguous, did not support any real changes in civil rights, despite a 'less hostile' system of slavery – an intriguing paradox. A comparison of the American and Brazilian slavery systems highlights their differences but also confirms the complexity of both social dynamics. This social complexity enforces the need to understand not only what happened, but also how it happened – and especially how it affected and deepened the inequality of the Brazilian society of today.

Healing the Wounds and Moving Forward

In psychology the process of acknowledging a traumatic experience enables both individual and collective growth. Coming to terms with our slavery past is not just a Brazilian theme – European countries that took part in slavery have had to deal with the issue too. During the transatlantic slave trade, Denmark was involved in the transport of around 100,000 slaves from Africa to the former West Indies. Yet this period of colonialism is generally not present in the Danish understanding of their history. As a result, says Astrid Nonbo Andersen, a Danish PhD researcher in the politics of remorse and apology, there is no pressure from the Danish people. She says: "Apologies from states are very rarely given without a period of pressure from the people, or from the outside world". She also argues that, "the refusal of the governments involved is a disrespect, it is like telling the descendants of the victims of the Nazi regime that their history didn't matter" (Madsen, 2012).

It is understandably painful to remember certain historical events. On the ships men and women were crowded between decks in the dark, without sanitation, without running water, for at least 15 to 16 hours a day. Two men were chained together, as a rule the right ankle of one to the left ankle of another, in a space barely larger than a grave

Chapter 4: A Case of Resilience

(Tannenbaum, 1946). Only in 1684, after almost two centuries of slave trade, did the Portuguese pass a law that required captives to be given three meals and 2.6 liters of water a day, and medication. At the time, all captives were marked with a hot iron on the shoulder, thigh or chest, "a scene of how the slave was robbed of his human dignity" (Mattoso, 1996).

No one person can be judged responsible for such an atrocity. The political context, economic interests, and poor human mentality kept slavery alive for centuries – for exactly 338 years in Brazil, an overwhelming proportion of the five centuries since the arrival of the Portuguese.

Illegal French ship in 1882, transporting African slaves. Photo by Marc Ferrez

In my research I have found no record of any official apology by the Portuguese, French, Spanish, Danish or Swedish to those Africans forced into slavery. The US parliament made an official apology for slavery in June 2009, six months into Barack Obama's presidency. A similar discourse happened in the Netherlands in June 2013, which saw experts, representatives of various social organizations, and members of the Antillean and Surinamese communities coming together in parliament to discuss the Dutch role in slavery. It has been reassuring to hear Glenn Helberg, chairman of the Consultative Body for Dutch Caribbean (OCAN), assert that a formal apology is the first step, and that this should be followed by reconciliation and a broad dialogue on this shared history. Part of this process is to deal with the 'collective trauma' of the slavery past and 'feelings of superiority' – the source of the slave trade as well as a key factor in contemporary racism and discrimination. Helberg believes this vicious circle must be broken. He adds: "We should recognize that slavery was a crime against humanity. Let's look at our mindset, reconcile and work on a joint future" (*The Daily Herald*, 2013).

The British government, perhaps to avoid the possibility of having to provide financial compensation, has to date refused to offer any official apology for its role in the slave trade (although in 1999 Liverpool City Council did pass a formal motion of apology for the city's involvement in slave trading; the Church of England did likewise in February 2006). Although Britain may have led the way in bringing to an end the trans-Atlantic slave trade from which it had so profited, the need for an apology remains. Tony Blair, Prime Minister of the UK, did issue a statement of "deep sorrow" for Britain's role in the trans-Atlantic slave trade. According to CNN journalist Paul Sussman (2006), this was a business that, between the 16th and 19th centuries, forcibly transported an estimated 3 million black Africans across the Atlantic and into servitude in the New World.

Slavery was a large-scale forced migration process and people throughout Brazilian society (not to mention throughout the colonies) were complicit. To be a success the process required a developed trading and logistics structure. It required elaborate planning, technical resources and the financial motivation of everyone involved to implement the long process, from 'recruiting' people, keeping hundreds of them in captivity, transporting them over the Atlantic, delivering them to all regions from north to south, and selling them with a margin. It demanded a high level of intellectual development from those involved. It is about time government officials, as well as citizens, stopped sweeping the slave trade under the carpet; it is time to honestly face the facts and take responsibility for a truly liberated future. An apology helps in the process of recognizing this powerful historical event; it helps all parties involved, especially Brazilians, to assimilate consciously its consequences.

Chapter 5

The Colonial Legacy Today

Highlights

Brazil is not a cultural 'melting pot'.

◆

Ethnicity drives the dynamics of the 'ugly people' and the 'beautiful people' in Brazil.

◆

The colonial period's destructive legacy can be seen in family structure, social stratification, division of labour, and the educational gap.

Chapter 5: The Colonial Legacy Today

Turning the pages of the past in order to write about the Brazil of today has been a demanding task. Questions such as, "Have I covered all the important topics?" and "What have I missed?" still torment me. Whichever current view of Brazil I examined, it seemed incomplete, especially after having written about the invisible influence of the Amerindians and the resilience of the Africans. Shedding light on the hidden facets of Brazil, a country that goes beyond carnival, soccer and girls in small bikinis, remains my objective. In this journey, however, I realized that only disclosing the missing pieces was not sufficient to understand the whole.

Making the necessary connections between certain past events and how Brazilians think, live and work today often seems an impossible mission. How can we draw accurate conclusions in such a heterogeneous and complex society? The need to reinterpret and revise ideas about Brazil will therefore persist. There is often no right or wrong opinion; rather, it is an ongoing process of matching historical causes and possible consequences expressed in observable behaviours. Even when there are no clear and direct links, acknowledging the historical and socio-economic context is essential. The most important element in this process is to be open to all possible interpretations, thereby avoiding judgments, preconceived ideas and stereotypes.

Not a 'Melting Pot'

Brazil is known to be a multicultural society. As mentioned in *Chapter 1: The Intercultural Movement*, Brazil is a 'hard to mix' multicultural society rather than a 'melting pot'. In Brazil there are many 'pots', each with separate and distinct conditions, ethnicity, and (especially) education. Ribeiro (2000) argues that Brazil is torn apart by classes of "unmixable components". Some literature (specifically from the early 1930s) refers to Brazil as a "racial democracy", a term first advanced by Brazilian sociologist Gilberto Freyre (1998), because the intense racial mix often makes race untraceable (and therefore not so important). More recent studies, such as those by Skidmore (2010), argue that the predominantly white elite within Brazilian society merely promoted racial democracy "to obscure very real forms of racial oppression". I'm inclined to agree, for the social conditions required for a society to enable an even and fair mixing are certainly absent. As we discussed in the previous chapters, social rights, access to education, and the legal and welfare systems remain ineffective – and the consequences of chronic corruption, criminality, and narrow and short-term public policies continue to do damage. There seem to be two opposing driving forces behind our social dynamics: one that unites us as a nation and another that separate us into classes.

The 'Beautiful People' Versus the 'Ugly People'

How the different (original) groups integrated continues to determine who are '*gente bonita*' (the 'beautiful people') and '*gente feia*' (the 'ugly people'), definitions commonly used in the Brazilian Portuguese language to describe social class and ethnic origin based on appearance, and thus where they 'belong'. Even the various European immigrants, who arrived mainly in the late 1800s and early 1900s (when, as I argue, the core formation of the Brazilian society had already taken place), blended according to these social divisions. Germans, Italians, Syrians, Lebanese, Japanese, Polish, among many others, faced difficulties in adapting to the dualistic colonial social dynamics; they too had to find their place in the 'beautiful' or 'ugly' social categories.

This social categorization based on skin colour (and its associated attributions) has been a core reference point even at government level from the early 1900s. At that time, as well as the need for cheap labour, the Brazilian government looked towards a 'whitening' of the population. In 1945 the government issued a decree favoring the entry of European immigrants into the country: "In the admission of immigrants, the need to preserve and develop, in the ethnic composition of the population, the more convenient features of their European ancestry shall be considered." (Skidmore, cited in Graham, 1991). Somehow it seemed to them more desirable to facilitate a 'genetic purification' than to feed, protect and educate the majority of the existing mixed population. These ideas persist today in many political views.

Brazil's poverty and inequality have resulted largely from these kinds of ideologies, which support a dualistic mechanism and were established and maintained by a combination of factors: land ownership concentration; exclusivist large-scale economic activities (such as sugar, gold, coffee and cacao); the prohibition of education as a means to social control; the slavery system; and post-slavery policies and conditions. Although this combination was commercially successful in terms of colonial aims, it was also a formula for social inequality and backwardness and the failure to create a fair society for those people in the tropics (excluding the ruling elite, of course).

The legacy of the colonial past remains as vivid as ever in Brazilian society. Looking at the Brazilian culture from an outside perspective, however, is probably the best position from which to see the nuances between past and present. Understanding the context in which historical events (our past) impact on people's behaviours (in the present) continues to be a crucial underexplored link. In my search for explanations of the Brazil of today, I have thus far been looking back. Now I would now like to focus on intercultural dynamics of the present, ones that are typically intriguing (or confusing) for the foreigner in Brazil (and for Brazilians too!); namely, the Brazilian family structure, social stratification, the division of labour, and the educational gap.

Brazilian Family Structures

The implications of our colonial history on family structures are a good example of how historical events have a direct impact on social dynamics and how people interact with each other in the present. The nuclear family – that is, mother, father and children under one roof – cannot be assumed as the 'normal' family structure in Brazil. This is for a number of reasons. For example, marriage between slaves was often forbidden. Furthermore, the majority of the freed men and women did not belong to, and were not supported by, the kind of family structure most Westerners understand as 'normal' today. After gaining freedom came the struggle to find (unskilled) work and to buy a piece of land, and only then could people build a basic family unit.

Because slaves were considered an item of property, they could be moved at the will of the master; as a result, separation of families was common. As mentioned in *Chapter 5: The Colonial Legacy Today*, Africans were first separated from their ethnic groups on arriving in Brazil and mixed with those who spoke different African languages. Thereafter they could be bought and sold repeatedly, depending on the different economic cycles. In 1850, when slave trading (from Africa) became illegal, slaves were again separated during a massive transfer of manpower from economically depressed regions of the north and northeast (sugar plantations) to the southern and central regions in the mining regions. Children of slave mothers (even those whose biological fathers were the slave owners) were often left behind when their mothers were working at the plantation or back at the '*senzala*', the slave house, and looked after by others in the collective slave community; the elders usually took care of the younger members.

The above describes the social patterns of most of the population for four centuries. In a way it also explains how the Brazilian society of today was formed. Only the white minority had the luxury of having a stable family structure, often essential for fostering individuals into becoming constructive members of society. The lack of family structure also explains the important role of women in our society today, for they raised children alone, generation after generation. Although the African community-based structure did provide some support, these were communities of enslaved individuals with restricted possibilities and limited access to legal, educational and health systems. The nuclear family did not appear until quite late in Brazilian society for the majority of the population. This rather important fact, too, is often ignored.

As I noted in the previous chapter, during my childhood in Gurupi, in the State of Tocantins, I witnessed how the lack of government support created interdependence between those who own a piece of land and those who do not. Poverty has the potential to destroy families. My childhood playmate, Ana, was brought to live in my grandparents' house and expected to clean, iron and cook, as part of the 'agreement' made between my grandmother and her father in exchange for food, housing and the chance to attend school. (My grandmother even expected Ana to call her 'mother'. Ana refused, instead calling her 'godmother'.) Her family, who were from a poor rural area and had many mouths to feed, had given her away. Though she was young, she was old enough to understand the arrangement, but could do nothing to resist being separated from her family. I had the opportunity to get to know her well. We were only allowed to play, though, when she had finished her duties. This case makes a good example of this lasting Brazilian social dynamic in which living conditions depended exclusively on personal exchanges of favors.

Even though slavery does not exist anymore, this ambivalent kind of 'agreement' remains. For many years, I have wondered about Ana's life and how difficult it must have been to work for free most of her life (she remained until both my grandparents had died) and still be expected to be grateful. (Ana's story is not an isolated case.) As a child we learn to play the game, to survive, but in our hearts we never accept such unfair treatment. Whenever questioned, the adults would tell me that she should be glad for what she had; she was lucky to get away from poverty and to move to the city and study.

Today I realize how much my childhood memories resemble the structure of the old system. There were many families who were dependent on and lived around my grandfather's farming activities; some exchanged favors, and some offered services for 'food and protection'. This paternalistic arrangement can still be found in many rural areas in the central and northern parts of Brazil.

Social Stratification

There is more than just rich and poor to the Brazilian social structure. This traditional view of the emerging countries is an over-simplification. The complex stratification of today's Brazilian society can be seen as another legacy of colonialism, which created a hierarchic structure with layer upon layer. Even among slaves there were many different layers: newly arrived slaves who could not speak the local language; slaves born in Brazil (who were therefore familiar with the system and language); rural slaves (who probably had the worst conditions); slaves from the gold and diamond mines (who sometimes got lucky and could buy their freedom); urban slaves (who could perhaps learn a skill, and lived in close proximity to their masters); freed slaves (and those who were still paying for their freedom); and finally, the *mulatos*, or mixed blood, who often did not know where they belonged, but had limited access to both worlds. They all represented different socio-economic classes and had different functions in this society.

A woman being carried by her slaves, province of São Paulo in Brazil, ca.1860. These slaves, seen barefoot here, were likely in the lowest position in the social hierarchy. They were probably newly arrived from Africa and could not speak Portuguese; therefore they were given roles based purely on physical strength.
Photo by VASQUEZ, Pedro Karp. 2003

Some people still wonder today: "What is so bad about having been a colony?" They may ask: "What difference does it make that we had slaves in Brazil?" One of the consequences was the deepening of socio-economic inequality, meaning social relations were guided by differences, rather than commonalities. This was a system that hindered social mobility; it did so by ignoring education and reinforcing the chronic discrimination of black and indigenous peoples. It also idealized white Europeans, and any outsider, and regarded them as ideal.

Within the context of the colonial period and slavery a struggle for dignity was played out. Newly arrived slaves were often treated as *primitive creatures*. The picture above only hints at the significance of having access to clothes and shoes, or not – the difference between being barefoot or not was symbolically huge; to be a human being or not was always at stake. The struggle for dignity started as soon as a slave child was born. Young slaves could run freely and played with the white children until the age of about six; they experienced, to some degree, the privilege of freedom for a few years. After that they were strong enough to work and everything changed. "The child learned soon that the abyss between master and slave was unbridgeable" (Mattoso, 1996). A dark skin, especially one as dark as night, represented a social class with no social support, no land, no education, no housing, no family structure and, usually, no opportunity to learn a professional skill.

To understand the Brazil of today, its poverty, high crime rate, and social and educational backwardness, requires taking an honest look at our recent past. Again, for Brazilians, taking this step back means recognizing our origins; for foreigners in Brazil, it means developing empathy. Both are important for today's intercultural challenges. (I will discuss the role of empathy in business in the next chapter.)

Ambivalent Communication

Interactions in Brazil have always been characterized by social paradoxes and ambivalence. The Brazilian indirect communication style is a consequence of these social ambiguities rather than a conscious preference. It is a result of chronically unequal social relations imposed over the centuries and acts almost as a social survival mechanism. (The same indirect approach can be found in many other high context cultures, including India and China. We will discuss other similarities among high context countries in the next chapter). Survival is the driving force behind cultural behaviours like this.

Just like children, newly established societies have to learn how to survive ambivalent relationships, such as those between a slave and his master. In order to understand the coping mechanism developed by individuals to handle social irrationalities, it is worth differentiating between *paradox* and *ambivalence*. Paradox usually consists of two messages in which the first message is followed by an opposing message. Imagine you are

Chapter 5: The Colonial Legacy Today

driving and find a traffic sign which indicates that the road will turn to the right, but before any right turn appears, you find another traffic sign that indicates the road will turn to the left. A paradox necessarily implies two opposing messages.

Fig 3. Paradox: Two opposing messages

Ambivalence, on the other hand, consists of one message that contains opposing ideas. In developmental psychology the term 'ambivalent' is usually associated with attachment, a relationship between a child and the mother (or main caretaker). An *ambivalent attachment* occurs when the relationship is characterized by inconsistency – between what the mother says and what she does, so that the child feels confused. A child who has an ambivalent attachment is considered by many psychologists to experience the most harmful type of attachment, worse than an *insecure attachment* or *rejection*, because even if the latter hurt, it is better to know than to never know for sure (Bowlby, 1988). The impact of an ambivalent relationship will generally continue into adulthood.

Fig 4. Ambivalence: One message with two opposing ideas

Ambivalent communication derives from ambivalent relationships. I believe that today's indirect and implicit Brazilian communication style is a consequence of chronically ambivalent interactions historically. For example, in exchange for food and protection, slaves were expected to be submissive; their masters wanted them mostly to be "loyal, obedient and useful" (Mattoso, 1996). Cordiality and cruelty were entwined. The process of enslavement hid a deeper identity struggle for the slave. Part of this struggle is an internal conflict around meaning-making – between what is said and what the truth is. Slaves were forced to believe that to be black was to be a slave, but deep inside they must have felt that individuals of every colour had the right to be free.

The Brazilian slavery system left a deeply ambivalent imprint in our society, one that is often underestimated. Mattoso argues that, when slaves arrived in Brazil, "there was the phase of depersonalization, loss of individuality, when African captives – bought, sold, mortgaged, rented, and bequeathed, deprived of dialogue with their captors and the ability to express their own will – became beasts of burden, beasts that some doubted, despite the teachings of the Church, to be possessed of souls" (Mattoso, 1996). After being liberated, and thrown into society without assistance and/ or compensation, many generations of descendants of slaves continued to struggle for dignity. The process of adaptation to (or survival of) the demands of the unique dual-structure Brazilian society is gradual.

The Catholic ideology, which held together these ambivalent social interactions, has also contributed to the nature of how Brazilians communicate. The following quote by the Jesuit priest Vieira illustrates this:

> "Black brothers, the slavery you suffer, however hard and painful it may be, or seems to be, it is only half slavery. You are slaves in your exterior part, which is the body; however, in the other interior and noble half, the soul, you are not a slave, but free. When you serve your masters, you do not serve them as you serve men, but rather, as someone who serves God."

Brazilian slaves learned early on that the only guarantee of survival was to play the hypocritical game of the master. This relationship describes what Freud would call "the important early relationship", from which the Brazilian society still experiences a post-traumatic effect. This kind of relationship was imprinted in the subconscious of our people.

The Division of Labour

The division of labour in the colonial time still has an impact on the relations between social classes and the nature of work today. The social segregation between people who did manual work from those who did intellectual work remains. Young Brazilians from the elite (the so-called class A and B) would be ashamed to take a job in a fast food restaurant. This may sound strange to North Americans or Europeans, where part-time and side jobs are normal for students and young people. In Brazil, the nature of the work one does reveals the limits of one's social reach.

An example in my own life illustrates this distinction between work and class. When my husband, who is Swedish, used to cut the grass or do repairs on our house in Brazil, he was always questioned by our condominium guards: "Doctor, why are you doing that? We can arrange for someone to do it for you. You do not need to do that." This comment made my husband laugh, as he is not even a doctor.

The Education Gap

The educational gap left by the Portuguese colonial time is hard for most foreigners in Brazil to comprehend. In 1822, the year of Brazil's independence, two in every three Brazilians were slaves (black or Indian servants; and only one out of 10 people could read and write (Gomes, 2010). In 1889, the year Brazil became a republic, only 15 percent of the population could read and write; among blacks only one percent. Only 8000 people had a higher education (one in 1750 people), when the population was about 14 million. Until 1808 the press was forbidden in Brazil – in England, one person in 20 read the Sunday newspaper in 1850; in 1900, one in every three persons (Gomes, 2013). Thirty-eight percent of Latin America's illiterate population is Brazilian, most of them in the north and northeast.

Even compared to the other countries on the South American continent, the education gap is huge and will have consequences for many generations to come. By 1776 there were already nine universities in the US. The first university in Santo Domingo was created in 1538; in Peru and Mexico in 1551; and in Argentina in 1613. The first real Brazilian universities were only created around 1910 (University of Santa Catarina and University of Manaus). Before that there were only faculties of medicine (founded in 1829) and law (in 1826). Most of today's youth will still not be the first in their family to have a higher education. Most

Brazilians do not realize where these three centuries of educational delay come from and what they can do to compensate for such tremendous political irresponsibility. As mentioned previously, one of the greatest (and most sensitive) factors threatening our sense of national identity is the contrast between how large and rich we are in natural resources and yet how underdeveloped. This paradox reflects the essence of our national identity struggle and difficulty in asserting ourselves in the international arena.

The poor quality of education in Brazil (or should that be lack thereof?) inevitably has a significant impact on productivity and efficiency at work and is often cited as a risk factor for doing business in Brazil. This is the price to pay for years of shortsighted government policies. On an individual level, foreigners need to adjust their expectations of productivity and efficiency in Brazil to avoid being considered 'not sensible'. Learning how to deal constructively with mistakes and delays at work is crucial for developing business relations in Brazil. Ideally, being understanding and socially aware can be used to get closer to people and build trust. The way foreigners react to mistakes is one of the determinants of how Brazilians see them. As discussed in previous chapters, Brazilians have a love-hate relationship with foreigners, especially those from Europe and North America; however, demonstrating empathy and using mistakes as opportunities to develop relationships are essential to disentangling this complicated dynamic.

Chapter 6
Leadership Skills in Brazil

Highlights

International organizations in Brazil fail to calculate the cultural factor.

◆

Global leaders in Brazil must learn to transcend the ambivalence, aversion toward laws and regulations, and time orientation of the average Brazilian.

◆

The secret to building trusting relationships goes beyond 'the consistency between what you say and what you do'.

Now you know Brazilians do not see themselves as 'Latino' and that Brazil is not just an extension of Portugal, we can focus on the Brazilian business culture. The recent economic downturn has required global leaders not only to reassess their business strategy in this part of the world, but also their own set of competencies to get the job done in such a complex business culture. The apparent friendly environment can be misleading. Doing business in Brazil and managing effectively can be surprisingly tough – and quickly dispel the idealistic ideas of Brazil as a place of carnival, soccer and a beach lifestyle. The warm attention expat managers receive from Brazilians in the beginning of their assignment is usually only the first phase of an often complicated, though predictable, love-hate relationship.

International Organizations in Brazil

The strategic reasons of most international companies (North American, European and Asian), to have recently established themselves in Brazil usually involve exploiting our large and growing consumer market as well as setting up bases for expansion in the region. Unfortunately, few of these companies prepare sufficiently to manage the Brazilian way of working. Their failure to understand the cultural elements that colour communicating with, managing, and motivating their Brazilian staff can cause serious financial losses. Organizations tend to first eliminate all other possible causes – including problems with physical distance, technology, money invested – before considering cultural differences.

Recently, I went to China to assist a large Chinese company in understanding why things were not going according to plan in their Brazilian ventures; their 'unintentional mistakes' had caused them to lose millions of dollars. After our initial investigation it was clear they had neglected some of the most basic cultural elements of how Brazilians work. The most important question to ask a company having problems in Brazil is whether they have been aiming at getting *compliance* or *commitment* from their Brazilian counterparts. If companies only want their employees to follow executive orders, no specific management skills are required. In this case, companies may get employees to comply and obey, but without much personal involvement. This approach is possible but not, in the long term, for the best. It hinders motivation and creates mistrust, and leaders will fail to get the essential information they need to get the job done.

From a human resource perspective, supporting global leaders working in Brazil with the proper intercultural coaching could help them to adjust their expectations, and to balance between local needs and those of their headquarters. Leadership development researchers have long confirmed that, in general, traditional training works only between two to five percent of the time (McCauley & Van Velsor, 2004), and that a more strategic *learning from experience* approach – here defined as strategic organizational support for challenging assignments, adverse situations, and relationships – has the greatest impact (it is effective about 85 percent of the time). The failure to use the right combination of key intercultural competencies within the Brazilian culture can be costly, for there is usually a price to pay for not appropriately building relationships with major stakeholders and not fully engaging their local team members. Only organizations that fully understand the cultural context, and the need to develop these key intercultural competencies, have a chance of succeeding in this market.

An expatriate assignment in Brazil has immense potential to be a positive learning experience if combined with the developmental support necessary. Before exploring the competence framework required for leaders working in Brazil, the organization's selection process must choose leaders with soft skills and a genuine intention to engage with the local cultural context. Leaders whose sole intentions are to use 'copy and paste' strategies, implemented exactly as they were designed in their headquarters, and without considerable local adaptations, have little chance of success.

Global Leaders in Brazil

My first recommendation for foreign leaders in Brazil is to become familiar with the main challenges of the Brazilian business culture; namely, dealing with informal organization, learning to use negative feedback to build trust, and adjusting expectations. My second is to ensure you are truly accepted by locals as a leader. Understanding the similarities and differences between the Portuguese and Spanish sides of the continent and their uniqueness (as discussed in *Chapter 1: The Intercultural Movement*), cannot be underestimated; it can help global leaders to stand out by becoming 'regionally sensitive' – as a consequence they will be better accepted. However, knowing if you are accepted or not is the most difficult challenge, for Brazilians will not express their negative sentiments explicitly. The leader is usually the last to know how he/ she is perceived and what the real day-to-day organizational problems are.

A highly informal and indirect communication style characterizes the Brazilian business environment. This can easily be explained by the social dynamics of former colonial societies: more than 500 years of hidden corruption, inequalities, slavery and ambiguities have created the 'perfect' social conditions in which, in order to survive, people tend to form smaller parallel groups. These informal groups appear as a consequence of perceived power distance in the organizations. Informal groups are influential; it is in these groups that valuable information is shared and members support each other in the face of decisions perceived to be unrealistic. Together members dare to question laws and regulations and learn to say 'yes' when they mean 'no'. In order to deal with the informal organization and to influence it positively, global leaders need to take their time and dig into the deeper levels of the Brazilian cultural iceberg. They need to understand the ultimate link between cultural behaviours and profits/ losses.

Empathy

There are neither formulas nor shortcuts to becoming a true global leader. Working in Brazil, however, could be considered one of the final exams. It demands hard work to decipher the complexity of a society in which literacy levels have been low until recently or in which vast numbers of the population's history is steeped into poverty. Much has happened since those days, including military dictatorship and high inflation, but only recently – in 1984 – came the establishment of democracy. The purpose of understanding the historical and socio-economic context, however, only makes sense if it is transformed into empathy. Global leaders lead diverse human beings who are imperfect and make mistakes. Leading in Brazil demands empathy and all the soft skills one can have. Developing sensitivity to context, and especially knowing when to push and when to pull, is crucial if one is to emerge stronger from workplace crises and conflicts. Indeed, conflicts regarding delays and misunderstandings are common. The key to transcending these is to develop sensitivity to the informal context, and in so doing, build trust.

The 'Passion Button'

Our past teaches us that leaders should not expect blind obedience. This is what was expected of workers during the colonial times, and it has naturally caused much resentment. Many of my foreign clients comment on how energetic and positive the Brazilian employees appear to be. Even if this latent energy and willingness to help is typical of Brazilians, they are also perceived as rebellious. A common complaint from my clients is that Brazilians do not openly reject orders from superiors in the workplace. Rather, confrontation is avoided at all cost; there is often silent protest, usually taking form in a silent refusal to collaborate and share information. Brazilians insist on keeping crucial information within the informal organization; thus problems are not spoken of and it can be difficult for managers to identify or deal with them. This often leads to problems and delays.

It's no surprise, then, to hear my foreign clients say that they only become aware of issues near the end of a project, when deadlines are around the corner. The Brazilian tendency to keep important information within the informal groups, and to maintain harmonious social relations at all costs, can appear unprofessional to the outsider. This ambiguity, combined with a characteristically fluid concept of time, can drive foreigners crazy. Leaders who want to flourish in Brazil cannot afford to sit and wait for information to arrive. They must take a more proactive approach.

Leaders must also learn to harness the decision-making process by involving employees, even if (especially if) projects have been created elsewhere. If we take a closer look at the Brazilian working mentality, and specifically in relation to their approach to decision-making, we find many similarities with customs of the native societies. As explored in *Chapter 3: The Invisible Influence*, traditional small communities had a largely egalitarian social organization when it came to political decisions. Information handling was based on collective principles and focused on peer-to-peer relations. There was little power manipulation; in other words, there was no 'boss' who had the authority to give orders. The leader, who was admired for his/ her experience and charisma, did not make decisions alone.

My claim here is that we have the *invisible influence* (from the native peoples) regarding leadership preferences at play in the Brazilian workplace. In order to lead effectively in Brazil, one should make a clear distinction between the current leadership style and preferred leadership style. Organizations in Brazil are hierarchic due to the historical and socio-economic reasons discussed in this book. In my opinion, this hierarchy is not the preference. When international leaders understand this, they can use it in their advantage. It is necessary to take a step back in the decision-making process to create opportunities for employees to understand (and agree with) the reasons behind decisions. When I tell this to my clients, they often respond: "That is so childish and time consuming". I tell them to reflect on the costs of not doing this, especially the cost of delays, and the gains made when one gets full commitment from employees from the beginning of the project.

It is often wrongly assumed in international business that employees everywhere have the same motivations to work. The Portuguese understood the error of this thinking. As discussed in *Chapter 3: The Invisible Influence*, they soon realized a better approach was to become 'one of them'; only after that could they get full commitment from the locals to 'collaborate'. The different way in which the concept of 'work' is understood, and the values behind it, can trigger a range of problems in a multinational or foreign business operating in Brazil. Indeed, differences vary even between the southern and northern regions of Brazil. In the state of Amazon, for example, the Amerindian influence is arguably even more evident.

The population from the crowded urban areas in Brazil seems to have forgotten that, for traditional local societies who are still the backbone of the Brazilian society, the most desirable achievement each day was to be part of collective activities, such as finding as many resources as possible in order to share these with loved ones. Generosity and harmony were the most precious social values. It is perhaps no surprise then that the values considered most important by Brazilians are family, friendship, security and health, while the least important is power (Instituto Datafolha, 2010 and PNUD, 2010). Many of the aspirations and expectations of Brazilian employees of today are similar to those of our original peoples: full autonomy and the freedom to do as they believe is right. These aspirations (hidden to foreigners and often to Brazilians themselves), and a genuine willingness to help and contribute, are the implicit motivation behind the Brazilian passion – harnessing this will drive an employee's full engagement. This seems to be true even for those whose explicit motivation is to attain money to purchase goods and move up the social ladder. The challenge for international leaders lies mainly in learning to create genuine personal bonds that make work meaningful and give a reason to collaborate. A simple salary increase will never be enough. The best suggestion I have seen on how to make a true connection with people is to demonstrate that "you see them, you hear them and you validate them" (Brown, 2012); this is full empathy at work. Effective managers should not be afraid to go down the organizational levels to connect to the people that matter, those who influence the informal groups in the companies.

Informal Organizations

The idea that inequality and injustice are a 'normal' part of society, a commonly accepted ideology, remains a part of Brazilian reality. If international business leaders and managers want to effectively deal with indirect communicators in the Brazilian workplace, they need to have full empathy for the intentions behind the message, and not be fooled by the message itself. Chronically ambivalent environments tend to create and maintain informal organization. As we have seen, in the hierarchic Brazilian business world, ambivalence is incorporated into the nature of the communication style (indirect, implicit and highly contextual).

Ambivalence can also be expressed by a need to maintain informal organization, perhaps as a way to handle hierarchic organization, and as a silent form of resistance. A business case involving a Canadian multinational (in which I was involved as an intercultural consultant) illustrates perfectly the importance of taking seriously the differences in communication style. The Canadian company bought five factories in Brazil. As part of the integration process, the HR director for the Americas in Canada sent a 200-page employee handbook, which contained company HR policies and principles, to the HR managers of the factories. All the local HR managers confirmed they had received it, had no questions and would implement it. Six months later, it became clear that this handbook was never used, and no employee had heard about it. This business case is a good example of project implementation challenges in Brazil, especially where the project/ program is decided on or created at the headquarters without local involvement, a 'copy and paste' project – a project developed by 'outsiders'. Due to Brazil's colonial history, there is a tendency for Brazilians to resist and/ or reject ideas that are perceived to be 'imposed'. This resistance grows ever stronger in the informal organization, among peers, in the social chats by the coffee machine. In keeping with the Brazilian style of communication – indirect, implicit, and high context – employees will agree formally with higher management, but "Yes, I agree, I will do it" tends to mean, "I will think about and consider it."

Aversion to Laws and Regulations

The above-mentioned case of the Canadian multinational company reveals another element of Brazilian workplace behaviour: it should not be taken for granted that a 200-page employee regulation will be automatically respected. From a colonial historical perspective, written laws and regulations are not necessarily perceived as they are in the developed world; rather they may be perceived as 'not necessarily good, and not usually our laws'. In the Brazil of the recent past (last 500 years), personal and professional survival depended on the ability to *maneuver around* laws and regulations, also known as '*jeitinho brasileiro*' (the Brazilian way). In our history, most written laws and regulations were not created by the people and for the people. An example, and one mentioned earlier in this book, is that our first constitution, in 1824, did not even mention slavery, despite it being the reality for two-thirds of the population. In a recent survey conducted by FGV (2014), only 29 percent of Brazilians trust their judicial institutions. Obviously history should not be used as an excuse or justification to explain why people do not respect laws; however, respect for laws is usually the result of a long social development process. Though this is underway in Brazil, the automatic acceptance of regulations should not be taken for granted.

It should be clear by now that the colonial system, and how it kept slavery alive for almost four centuries via legal, economic and religious institutions, had a direct (and indirect) impact on the Brazilian society of today. A general aversion to laws and regulations is one of the most important consequences and is especially relevant for those seeking to do business in the country. It is understandably frustrating, especially for foreigners living in or visiting Brazil, to experience the Brazilian approach to law and regulations, but worth remembering what underlines the Brazilian collective consciousness regarding laws: they are not necessarily something positive. Brazilians still do not have respect for laws – a traffic stop sign is just one good example. Historically, laws have been made mostly *against* rather than for the majority of the population. Living for generations in a violent and unjust system, in which the most basic human rights were not guaranteed, kept social injustices alive for many generations. The unjust laws were made to protect the interest of the Church, and even to protect their source of income; in 1762, the costs for the services of a priest to baptize captives were about 7.5 percent of the price of sea transport from Africa (Mattoso, 1996). The state paid this expensive price to ensure ideological control and manipulation. Mistrust of laws and regulations continued even after independence in 1822, and has been further entrenched by military dictatorships (from 1964) and chronic government corruption which is still common today. As a consequence, the majority of the population often views legality as absurd, unfair and cruel; laws are constructs that have never protected them.

In the US the constitution is admired and respected; it became a concrete symbol of justice and is kept in a special, secure place in Washington and in the American people's hearts. In Brazil laws are not a reflection of the society's needs and struggle for justice. Thomas Jefferson stated, "All humans are born equal", but in Brazil the reality was very different. Brazilians have had to learn to deal with ambivalent laws and regulations, which did do not represent a process of legal and democratic consensus. Laws are, in many cases, contradictory, and consequently, not reinforced.

In our society exceptional courage was necessary to overcome injustice and achieve some degree of social order. Surviving *in spite of the laws* (instead of with the protection of the law) became a necessity; the need to find ways around the law prevails. Unfortunately, this mentality has gone to the extreme in our society.

Time Relevance

The difference in how humans perceive and experience time varies greatly among cultures and usually reveals how people attempt to control and organize their lives, and to make it predictable. The cultural definition of time can also be a symbol of how people show respect to each other. Many interculturalists have explored these differences: Trompenaars (1997) talks about the 'fluid' and 'exact' aspects of time; Hall (1976) differentiates between monochromic (doing one thing at a time) and polychromic aspects (doing several things at a time); and Hofstede and Minkov (2010) emphasize how some cultures differ in long-term and short-term perspectives. Another aspect of time should be emphasized if we are to understand the role of time (and punctuality or deadlines) in Brazil: *time relevance*.

Today we know that the idea of time assumed in most developed (Western) countries – that time is exact and sequential and that 'time is money' – does not apply everywhere in the world. In the Brazilian culture the concept of time shows not only social class (and urban versus rural) distinctions, but also how time-related issues are used to build trust.

Anyone who has had contact with the Brazilian culture knows that punctuality is not our strong point (with exceptions of course). But I do not want to analyze whether being punctual is good or bad, nor do I want to try to find historical explanations for differences (*Chapter 3: The Invisible Influence* touched on the indigenous people's concept of time). My intention is to introduce into our discussion two psychological mechanisms underlying the differences between cultures that focus on time (high time relevance) and cultures that do not focus on time (low time relevance).

With the demands of the modern world it is practically impossible to survive without keeping track of time, since *time is all we've got*. We cannot really imagine a life in which we ignore time and we would probably judge people who do this as primitive, inefficient and not sensible. Even though time is a focus of most people today, there is nonetheless a difference in how *relevant* time is for different societies and its consequence for how we experience life. In Brazil it is true also that time relevance differs between people's private and professional lives. In general, research in the field of psychology of time has confirmed that the brain uses two different mental cognitive processes depending on whether, in an experimental situation, it is required to do a task focusing on time or not (Grodin, 2008).

In one study reviewed by Zakay (2013), the first group of participants was asked to evaluate how much time had passed since they had finished a particular task (they did not focus on time during the task only afterwards). The researchers found that subjects experience *retrospective timing*, a mental process based on memory. In this case, the harder the task (more complex versus simpler math exercises, or greater intensity of information), the slower participants perceived time to pass. In other words, if we do not focus on time (low time relevance) and instead focus on the task, we perceive time to pass slowly; the actual chronological passage of time is shorter than we perceive it to be.

This mechanism can explain why people in low time relevance cultures (usually cultures from socially complex and highly heterogeneous societies), like Brazil and India, perceive time, to a certain extent, to be plentiful, fluid and dynamic (this appears to vary depending on what one is doing). This also explains people's impression that, when they are busy dealing with tasks in a (socially) complex environment, 'time flies'. Low time relevance is a cultural value, for in these high context cultures, the focus is usually on people and relationships (rather than on time). We have all experienced these kinds of moments, when we are so involved in what we are doing (usually when we are enjoying ourselves) that time seems to slow down, disappear, or even stop. Some psychologists call these moments 'flow'.

The first major study of the concept of flow was undertaken in the 1960s by Mihaly Csikszentmihalyi, today considered the 'founder of flow'. He became fascinated by artists, especially painters, who became 'lost' in their work. These artists got so immersed in their work they would disregard their need for food, water and even sleep. Flow has been experienced throughout history and across cultures, but low emphasis on time seems to be more typical, as mentioned, in high context cultures (such as India, China and Brazil). The teachings of Buddhism and Taoism speak of a state of mind known as the 'action of inaction' or 'doing without doing' that greatly resembles the idea of flow. Indian texts on Advaita philosophy, such as *Ashtavakra Gita*, and the Yoga of Knowledge, such as *Bhagavad-Gita*, refer to a similar state. According to researchers, when someone is in the flow state, he or she is completely involved with the task at hand. Without making the conscious decision to do so, one loses awareness of all other things: time, people, distractions, and even basic bodily needs. In summary, if we ignore time and focus on the tasks (and have fun), time seems to slow down.

In contrast, our brain perceives time very differently if we focus mainly on time (what typically happens in the Western or developed world). In the study mentioned earlier, the second group of participants were told they would have to evaluate the duration of time after the exercise (*prospective timing*), thus making time relevant during the exercise. A number of changes occurred. Firstly, participants based their evaluations on what researchers call an *attention cognitive* process (instead of memory). Secondly, the harder the task the *quicker* participants perceived time to pass. In other words, if we focus on time, and the more complex the task is – in terms of difficulty, interruptions, or changes in the environment or emotions (typical interactions in high context cultures such as Brazil and India) – the quicker we perceive time to pass. In summary, if we focus on time, we do not seem to fully appreciate what happens in our environment (since our brains are focused on keeping track of time) and, consequently, we hinder flow (we spoil the fun) and time appears to speed up.

Even though this research was not designed with cross-cultural situations in mind, it has helped me widen my understanding of the mechanisms underlying differences in time perception. It has also helped me to empathize with the frustrations that arise when people from different time relevance cultures interact. Each person's brain is supposed to function the same way, and we all can choose to focus on time or not, but we do not seem to be aware of having a choice, and the impact it has on how we experience time. One of the most common complaints I hear from my clients, who are mostly foreigners working in Brazil, are the everyday frustrations involved in dealing the 'Brazilian ability to ignore time' and expect everyone else to do the same.

I intentionally choose the words 'ability to ignore time', which can be a 'positive ability', rather than 'the inability to be punctual', because it helps us understand this difference in a non-judgmental way and as a learned behaviour or habit. Brazilians are usually perceived to be disrespectful, even rude, regarding punctuality. For many years I have searched for a way to explain to my foreign clients and friends

Chapter 6: Leadership Skills in Brazil

how it feels to live your day without looking at your watch. I have never succeeded. Although I am not a good example of someone who has this ability to 'ignore time' – most of my friends think I am 'Germanic' when it comes to punctuality – this research did help me acknowledge and appreciate the difference. Time relevance is a reflection of how people approach life and it offers another perspective for understanding intercultural interactions.

It is understandably difficult for someone coming from a high time relevance culture to work in Brazil. Usually, to them, there does not appear to be any advantage to letting go of time. But if we manage not to judge people based on how they handle time, we can see that there are other abilities associated with the 'ability to ignore time': the ability to be flexible, the ability to improvise, the ability not to (have to) be in control, the ability not to expect others to be in control, and especially the ability to go with the flow. From a native Brazilian point of view, living life free from the need to possess and control time was natural (at least this is how it was for thousands of years before the colonial period). Yet we are expected not to hold this view of time in our modern civilization. Perhaps this is due to an inability to understand that time can indeed be plentiful. It helps to see it from the Amerindian perspective: after about 12,000 years of not prioritizing time, they were suddenly required to be on time – for Mass, when the first missionaries built their churches and rang their bells. Before that, time was like the endless flow of a river, which would pass by and be measured in days and nights.

In the corporate world it is obviously impossible to ignore time. One of the challenges of doing business in Brazil is therefore to learn how to handle the excessive 'flexibility' involved in getting things done by the agreed time, as well as to unravel the Brazilian approach to time and, as a consequence, our planning skills. This was first pointed out to me by a cosmopolitan client from a major Italian company based in Brazil, who said, "I often wonder what is more confusing: to deal with delays, lack of organization, or lack of planning." As an intercultural coach (and as a Brazilian), this was probably one of the most difficult behaviours to explain. I wanted to find a good historical justification for this Brazilian behaviour, but instead found myself quickly apologizing for it. Luckily, instead of taking the pathway of blame, we both agreed to take one step at a time. We focused on what she could do to adapt to this behaviour and, at the same time, we explored the values involved in her own approach to time management, planning and communication – and finally, we could discuss how time concept impacts on building trust in the Brazilian culture.

Building Trust

In Brazil, if someone (especially a service worker) tells you that they will be at your house at 2 pm, it usually means that 'they will do the best they can to be there at 2 pm, but in case this does not happen, they are counting on you to trust that they did the best they could'. Agreeing on a specific time often does not always mean the person will be there; it just means there is an intention and that flexibility is expected. The funny (and often tragic) thing about how Brazilians handle time is that, in this case, trust is not based on the person's ability to be punctual; it is based on the ability of the person who had to wait to be flexible. Building trust in Brazil therefore requires an understanding of each other's expectations around your agreement.

High levels of trust are believed to be one of the best indicators of a country's well being (Weiner, 2008). Trust is the foundation for any harmonious human interaction; it is not optional, and it is often a matter of survival. Building trust with people from high context cultures like Brazil is, without doubt, the most difficult challenge for foreigners in both private and professional situations, because it confronts social economic, ethical and moral norms. Some people doubt if trust is even possible, as individuals from these cultures have difficulty (or a different way) of saying "no". As we have already discussed, their communication is highly indirect and contextual. Even when they agree to something, they might not really mean what they say. But is trust more or less important in those cultures? Is there a formula to tell if you can trust a Brazilian or not? There are no simple answers but let me try to make a contribution that will improve understanding of what lies beneath the surface.

An American woman (married to a Brazilian man) once told me about one of her biggest disappointments with the Brazilian concept of committing to plans, which occurred while planning her wedding party. She already knew their Brazilian friends and relatives were "kind of difficult" when it came to making a commitment, so, in order to avoid misunderstandings, she called each guest (after she had sent out the invitations) to confirm if they were really coming. She needed to know the exact number of guests, because they had a budget to keep to and because she knew many of them lived far away and would need additional hosting. (This happened before software applications to organize events existed.) She described how everyone she talked to on the phone was friendly and happy about the invitation; they all sounded optimistic about attending. To make a long story short, only 40 percent showed up.

Building trust can also be complicated in professional contexts. The case of the Canadian company, demonstrates that 'silence' can also be misleading and can cause costly delays in project implementation. When the HR managers were told to implement a new policy they did not really agree with, they merely ignored it. In this case, consideration must be given not only to the Brazilian aversion to rules and regulations, but also to their difficulty in saying "no". To be direct and to the point, especially when a situation involves a disagreement, is considered rude in Brazil. However, in the situation faced by both the American woman planning her wedding and the Canadian company, other Brazilians would either have 'interpreted' the answer as a "no", or they would have understood the context. Again, here trust is allocated to the listener's 'ability to read the context' rather than the speaker's 'inability to mean exactly what they say'.

Even though building trust in cultures like Brazil is complicated for foreigners, 'the ability to read the context' is a matter of survival. When people communicate in a direct and straightforward way and they mean every word they say (as in most developed countries), building trust is much easier and simpler. The definition of trust, implicitly agreed upon, in these countries as being 'the consistency between what people say and do' works (for the most part) in those cultures. We can compare learning to build trust with driving a car: if you can drive in violent and frenetic Brazilian (or Indian) streets, driving in the calm streets of Sweden will be a piece of cake. If you learn to read between the lines and interpret the context in an accurate way in a Brazilian environment, you can most probably build trust and survive socially anywhere in the world.

Trust is key for any successful human interaction, but even more so in *volatile, uncertain, complex* and *ambiguous* (VUCA) cultures than in any other cross-cultural collaborations. There are even trust assessments, such as the International Team Trust Indicator (ITTI) by Worldwork, which is designed to help international teams increase performance based on nine main indicators as well as 45 factors identified to impact on trust. According to Richard Lowe and Geraldine Pace, the creators of ITTI: "Trust is never binary; and it is never simply off or on". They argue that trust is always relative to what we expect from others and what we actually get; it is a multi-faceted decision-making process, which means there are many different indicators that lead to the decision to trust or not. However, in the case of the Brazilian culture, the skills required to build trust are among many others, including: to see the invisible (to have enough information of the context and values involved); to build bridges by learning to use and interpret the right verbal and non-verbal communication; and, finally, to deal with mistakes and delays in a constructive way.

Dealing with differences in a constructive way is easier said than done, but this is what intercultural relations are all about. Having knowledge about a specific country and its history alone is never enough. Learning to make connections between past and present, to understand context, is an art. Cultural clashes hurt; our gut reactions are often too quick to control. It seems 'natural' to make judgments and reinforce stereotypes instead of taking a deep breath and time to reflect, or look inward. Hopefully, our discussions about some of the more common Brazilian cultural issues (such as ambivalence, the aversion to laws and regulations, and time relevance) have helped you to build your overall knowledge about the Brazilian culture and shown the need to develop some specific skills.

Chapter 7
An Emerging Cultural Approach

Highlights

The high context cultural aspects of the BRICS countries have different root causes.

◆

Intercultural exchange sparks self-awareness only if it is done from an even position of power.

◆

The right proportion of intellectual, emotional and spiritual intelligence ensures survival and defines culture.

Chapter 7: An Emerging Cultural Approach

Globalization and the recent international economic crisis have contributed to shaking the preconceived ideas of west and east, north and south. For developing countries, both BRICS (Brazil, Russia, India, China and South Africa) and MIKT (Mexico, Indonesia, South Korea and Turkey) have brought in changes so intense that the world seems upside down. BRICS and MIKT cluster their respective countries according to 'economic potential', which originally referred to markets that are "supposed to provide greater potential for profit, but also more risk from various factors" (Wikipedia). In a way, their shared similarities created an opportunity to receive the attention (and investments) they need. At the same time, an opportunity has been created for them to reassess who they are and who they want to be as nations.

For these societies globalization represents another top down push for them to reposition themselves in the international arena. Western companies from mature markets are going after the new middle class consumers in the emerging markets. This effort seems to be particularly conflicting for the emergent societies because, even if they have a strong drive to catch up and fit in, changes occur too rapidly. The particularities of this group of countries, especially the heterogeneity and the complexity of their societies, deserve, in my opinion, a dedicated approach in the study of their cultures. Interculturalists from all backgrounds (anthropologists, linguistics, economists, historians and psychologists) have attempted to contribute to international political conflicts and to support global environmental collaboration, but a lot is still to be done.

In their search to understand the formation and impact of culture in international relations, intercultural researchers started from complex and more complete cultural models yet moved recently into simplistic computer applications which claim to prepare individuals to deal with other cultures and even avoid cultural shocks (if that is possible). It is acknowledged that we should move from giving knowledge and superficial information about a specific countries to helping individuals to develop their self-awareness and skills to handle intercultural interactions, yet we still struggle to do so. As discussed in the previous chapter, the causal relationships between past events and present behaviours are often hard to pinpoint. We intuitively know, for example, that Brazil's current social inequality was partially caused by our colonial history, but for how long can our colonial past be blamed for the current social status? And which other factors are involved?

Embracing a Dynamic Concept of Culture

On my journey to study the Brazilian culture I came across an anthropological masterpiece called the 'Systems of Culture' schema, created in 1953 by Edward Hall and George L. Trager. In this thorough matrix they include all (or almost all) elements of culture: the formal, informal and technical levels as well the core system, orientational, expressional and material systems. The authors begin by considering linguistics before moving on to discuss culture as firmly based on pre-cultural biological activity. According to them, culture integrates various levels of complexity and only in taking into account the nature of these, and keeping them strictly apart, can the analysis of culture arrive at a clear picture.

It was with great contentment that I explored the depth of their model and its content, levels, structure and systems. Most of all, I appreciated the dynamic nature of their concept of culture, which was developed as an attempt to apply science to support international peacemaking efforts in the post World War II period. Their work inspired me to continue looking for even better ways not only to explain culture, but also to help everyday individuals from different cultural backgrounds to understand each other.

The focus of this book (which is not academic), is not to solve such difficult tasks in the intercultural field. Neither is this book – yet – a means to publish the findings of my own empirical research in social psychology. The aim of this chapter is rather to call attention to the need to take into account the uniqueness of each culture from its own perspective (and not only from a Western – that is, North American and European – perspective). As well as allowing me to express my frustration about how Brazil is perceived, writing this book meant I could present some alternative views. In this chapter I emphasize the importance of the following:

1. The mechanisms that link the historical and socio-economic context to a particular cultural behaviour seem to follow a pattern and must be better understood. Social welfare systems (and the lack of them) seem to be at the centre of culture formation. It is necessary to go deeper into the living conditions that created any given cultural behaviour and particularly what it took to survive in that context. An important consideration here is that people do not always consciously choose their behaviours (or have cultural 'preferences'), as mentioned in the previous chapter. Rather, behaviours are often an unconscious

consequence. Survival and culture are closely related. Even though there is a clear shift from survival to self expression values in more developed countries (according to World Value Survey), the quality of welfare systems, legal systems, democratic history and level of citizenship rights have a significant impact on how people interact with each other, how they interact with the environment and what strategies they develop to survive. Simplified cultural dimensions are clearly insufficient and even |misleading when explaining complex cultures.

2. Any culture-related observation must take into account, firstly, who the observer is, where he/ she comes from, and his/ her international exposure. Secondly, the direction of the intercultural movement must be acknowledged; that is, one must consider the difference between the socio-economic backgrounds of the observer versus the culture being observed. As explained in *Chapter 1: The Intercultural Movement*, in the Intercultural Movement Model, the direction of the movement affects people's attitude and expectations and the nature of intercultural interactions.

3. There is a clear need to integrate history, economics, philosophy, anthropology and psychology. Only a multidisciplinary task force can identify a common thread and construct a more comprehensive cultural understanding.

I tried to apply the above when looking at the Brazilian culture. I have long realized that the first 'cultural clash' that people from a developed country face when they arrive in Brazil (or in any other developing country), is to accept poverty and social inequality as a 'normal' part of society. The most frequent unspoken question is: "How can people (and their government) not do anything about such living conditions?" A lot goes on in a person's mind even before they have made any contact with a local person. Actually, a lot goes on in both people's minds before any interaction; this is a game in which expectations, stereotypes, attitudes, and individual background are the main players.

Brazilians usually see themselves as warm, friendly and happy people and they consider *gringos* (mostly from North America and North Europe)to be *cold*. On the other hand, *gringos* see Brazilians as *cold* because they appear to be negligent about social inclusion. This is a classic clash between developed and developing world ideas of what it is to be warm or cold. Brazilians, especially those who have never been abroad or have not personally experienced a more equal and fair society in which everyone's basic rights are guaranteed, usually interpret this kind of 'typical *gringo* comment' as arrogant and over-judgmental.

It is generally accepted that, in the process of becoming interculturally competent, *self-awareness* is the first step. Every human interaction is like looking at a mirror. If the mirror is placed correctly – parallel to the person, in such a way the person sees himself/ herself – he/ she can literally see 'eye to eye'. In this position, eye contact triggers self-reflection, which triggers self-awareness. However, if the mirror is placed so that a person does not see the reflection of his/ her own image, the process of self-awareness is hindered. If they look up at or look down on another, they put themselves in a superior or inferior position, and the intercultural interaction remains skewed. An uneven positioning also influences on one's perspective, which is defined as a mental position from which one views others from a certain angle, where more or less positive or negative qualities are more salient (Montgomery, 1994). We let our expectations and beliefs direct our perceptions, so that we confirm what we already "know" (Allport, 1954).

In the psychological field, we know that asymmetric interactions between strong and weak individuals (with respect to power relations) can predict behaviours (Coleman, 2012). According to Deutsch and Kelley (cited in Coleman, 2012) power relations, conflict orientation and attitudes remain relatively stable for long periods of time and become internalized and chronic over time (Coleman, 2012). Since early in our contemporary history, social interactions in Brazil happened from uneven power positions; the result was *cultural appropriation* (or the assimilation of the white man's culture) instead of true cultural exchange. This is probably the same for all early interactions of any other colonized country.

Another way to be aware of one's own culture is to look at it from a different perspective, or from an outsider's point of view. Changing perspectives is another good reason why travelling and interacting with other cultures is so stimulating. For many people, returning home from a trip abroad often brings an 'aha' moment, a crucial moment of comparison that enables you to really see yourself and your country from an outside perspective. It is a pity that these moments are not long lasting. When Brazilians return home from a trip to America or Europe, they are forced to see a reflected image of an unequal society which is no longer 'normal' to them. The reflection of social negligence becomes clearer, but they also confirm their comforting perception

Chapter 7: An Emerging Cultural Approach

of coming home to their people's warmth. For Westerners (North Europeans and North Americans especially), changing position might provide the opportunity to expand their horizon beyond the materialist, ordered, and controlled way of being, and to accept and validate complexity, 'chaos', situations beyond one's control and the unpredictable values these emerging countries bring to the table. The process of self-awareness is only the first step before one can really learn to take advantage of this diversity, and bridge and integrate differences. Another sensible consideration when studying the emerging cultures is to avoid applying overly categorized cultural dimensions (such as individualism versus collectivism, hierarchic versus egalitarian, etc.). These dimensions have made an invaluable contribution to the intercultural field, but should be applied with caution. We must look deeper into what has caused such behaviours to exist in the first place. This is especially true if we compare two cultures of two developing countries.

A comparison between Germany and China, a developed country and a developing country, based on cultural dimensions of individualism/ collectivism and low/ high hierarchy can be very interesting and helpful. However, when comparing cultures from two developing countries, for example, Brazil and Mexico or South Africa and China, cultural dimensions are less insightful and can even lead to further misunderstandings mainly because they ignore historical and ideological differences.

In order to understand the emergent countries, we must dig into the sea of complexity and look for further reasons that caused them to be complex. Complexity, which as we now know is usually described as *high context* in the intercultural field, can have different root causes. Therefore we must look more seriously into the differences in ideologies, as well as historical and socio-economic aspects, to have a more complete picture. According to traditional interculturalists, such as Hofstede (2005) and Trompenaars (1997), Mexico, Brazil, and China, have *hierarchic, indirect communication*, and *high power distance* cultures; however these definitions are insufficient to help a Chinese person do business in Brazil, because they too are hierarchic, indirect communicators and have high power distance in their organizations. While the Chinese hierarchical structures are based on the Confucianism ideologies, the Brazilian hierarchic structures are based on social economic inequalities. Both nationals communicate indirectly but in completely different ways.

The emerging countries have in common highly complex and contextual societies; what makes each society so complex, what holds people together and defines how they interact, is essentially different.

In other words, the ideologies supporting their complexity vary. These societies reflect an internal dynamic mechanism – they have a reason and logic of their own. Instead of exploring this logic or ideology to explain these cultures, interculturalists tend to simplify them merely as high context.

Chaotic... or Non-Linear?

From a Westerner's (or outsider's) perspective, high context societies can be perceived as disordered, messy and 'chaotic'. Dr. Devdutt Pattanaik, an Indian Doctor in Mythology, offers a fascinating and more comprehensive approach to exploring culture: he acknowledges the Western difficulty to understand the 'chaotic' Indian society as the former's tendency to put order into place and keep control. According to him, in the Western ideology (both Greek and biblical) chaos is the absence of human control and, in order to become 'civilized', a society needs to control everything as much as possible. By doing so, however, these societies limit diversity instead of allowing for people to be different.

From a Western perspective, Brazil is also 'chaotic'. The Brazilian culture shares with the cultures of other emerging countries what some mathematicians in the study of chaos theory would call a *non-linear* (social) *system*; a highly unpredictable system, such as weather and climate, where "the output is not directly proportional to the input" (Kellert, 1993). Chaos theory is an interesting field of study, which includes disciplines such as meteorology, sociology, physics, economics, biology, and philosophy. This field of study might also help us to understand the unpredictable behaviours in 'chaotic' cultures and to confirm the need to investigate our past more systematically. Investigating the our past, however, is much easier in China or India because they rely on the 5000-year history, where mythology or millenary traditions are preserved; in Brazil, in contrast, we must still rely on insights of the non-written history to help further explain our culture.

Research literature explains that the technical difference between a *chaotic* and a *non-linear* system (such as those of complex countries like Brazil and India) is that the non-linear system is *history dependent* (Kellert, 1993). In reality, the term 'non-linear' is a more appropriate as there are, technically speaking, no chaotic countries. In the emerging countries, understanding how people interact with each other and with their environment, and how people develop strategies to survive, are even more determined by socio-economic and historical facts than anything else. Consequently, these socio-economic and historical factors have a great chance of explaining what we see.

Another important reason why the study of high context cultures needs an additional approach is because of the ethnocentric biases inherent in Western dominance of scholarly ideas, specifically in the field of social sciences. Most of the scientific research about human behaviour and cognition, as well as attempts to define the universal human nature, is produced in the Western or developed countries, using data mostly from Western participants, which may not be valid in other cultures. Researchers are at risk of drawing conclusions based only on *Western, educated, industrialized, rich* and *democratic* (WEIRD) societies (Henrich, Heiner & Norenzayan, 2010).

A 2008 survey of the top six psychology journals, for example, shows that more than 96 percent of the subjects tested in psychological studies from 2003 to 2007 were Westerners – with nearly 70 percent from the US alone. That is, 96 percent of the subjects in these studies came from countries that represent only 12 percent of the world's population (Watters, 2014). Recent research done by the anthropologists Heine, Norenzayan and Henrich (in Watters, 2013) has shown that culture influences cognition as well as the way people think and behave. Ideas previously thought to be universal by researchers may just be Western ideas.

Henrich' s research in Peru with the indigenous Machiguenga population, and in 14 other small-scale societies in locations from Tanzania to Indonesia, shows that differences in spatial reasoning, the way we infer the motivations of others, categorization, moral reasoning, boundaries between the self and others, and other arenas were not genetic, but cultural. Henrich focused on the different ways people in Western and Eastern cultures perceive the world and the differences in how they understand themselves in relationship to others (Watters, 2013). Yet guided by ideas of Western ethnocentricity, researchers tend to conclude that experiments using participants mostly from western cultures are valid for the whole human population. This seems to be the case not only in how history is written, but also in the theories of the fields of economics and psychology.

Another good example of an attempt to study culture from the point of view of the emerging countries is Subaltern Studies, a postcolonial theory of anthropology. The concept of *subaltern* has been used by South Asian, Indian and South American scholars to describe excluded mass populations (lower classes and the ethnic groups), namely those at the margins of society. This term defines these populations not in relation to the dominant (hegemonic) culture, but rather in their own terms and in relation to others in a similar position around the world. The word *subaltern* was first mentioned by the Italian Marxist, Antonio Gramsci (1891–1937), before being elaborated on by the scholarship of Eric Stoke and Ranajit Guha, to describe narratives of the history of India and South Asia. The Latin American Subaltern Studies Group was founded in 1993 by five academics (John Beverley, Robert Carr, Jose Rabasa, Ileana Rodriguez and Javier Sanjines). In general, they study the "continued dominance of Western ways of knowing, and of intellectual enquiry" (Latin American Subaltern Studies Group, 2006).

What I call the *emergent cultural approach* is not necessarily a new approach to study culture, but rather a call for caution applying existing Western-biased ideas. On a personal level, it is a call for attention to the need to respect and include local knowledge developed by authors in all relevant disciplines, which, in most cases, is only available in the local language(s).

The *emergent cultural approach* I envisage can be seen as an *ethno-relative* (as opposed to *ethnocentric*) approach. *Ethnorelative* is a term introduced by Milton Bennett (1993), which refers to an approach that validates cultural differences from their own perspectives. The following diagram summarizes the key elements of the *emergent cultural approach*.

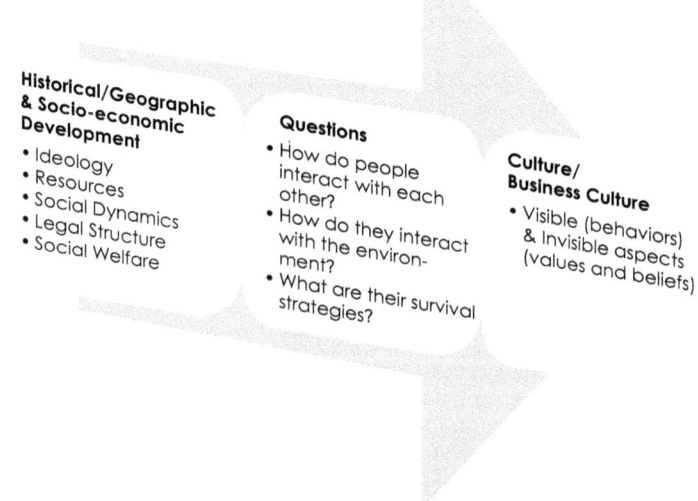

Fig 5. The Emergent Cultural Approach

Having this integrated structure in mind enables us to guide our search from specific historical and socio-economic elements to specific cultural behaviours. Constructing this link helps us understand the nuances of complex cultures. For example, abundance and scarcity of resources affect not only how people interact with the environment and with each other, but also what survival strategies they adopt. The need to rely on rational, emotional, social, spiritual or ecological intelligence in order to survive can vary according to that society's unique challenges. In some countries, individuals facing food scarcity (whether due to geographical factors, weather or war) are forced to develop order, control and predictability; this becomes a matter of life and death.

For example, the native population from the Andes had completely different environmental challenges in the pre-colonial period than the native population in the east of the Amazon. Either way, survival efforts required a focus on rationality, organization, interaction with the environment, and traditional knowledge. In other cultures survival efforts may require closer social ties and integration. In others still, a high level of emotional intelligence is required, and how emotion is incorporated in the verbal and non-verbal communication will determine success and survival. There are endless possible 'right' combinations depending on each context, the cultural diversity of the European continent, where the contrast between the South and the North is huge, would be another perfect example to explore this idea.

Rational, Emotional, Ecological and Spiritual Intelligence

Countries like Brazil and India have had thousands of years of ancestor worship, worship of nature, and complex daily spiritual rituals; survival has often required a transcendent and expansive view of life. In this respect we have a lot in common, although this diverse spiritual dimension is more visible in India, where the richness of religious mythology has been better preserved. Nonetheless, this highly active spiritual life has a direct impact on the formation of concepts like time, ambition, and success.

The exact proportion and focus given to *rational, emotional* and *spiritual* intelligence in a society are intertwined with their historical and socio-economic realities. The key point here is to incorporate all these elements in a more systematic way in the search to fully grasp the concept of a particular culture. Looking at the proportions of different kinds of Intelligences – rational, emotional, ecological and spiritual – that a society has learned to use in order to survive would be an interesting and more valuable way to study these cultures.

Despite access to prolific information online, the need to (re)elaborate the concept of culture from different perspectives and disciplines persists. As a psychologist, my tendency to see the world from this perspective is natural, but I still feel the need to integrate other areas of knowledge. We live in an era of 'consciousness', in which we are all able to exercise the frontal cortex of the brain responsible for meaning-making – what better way to do so than through stimulating intercultural experiences. This part of our brains works with metacognitive mental processes, whereby all the information available to us is stored and from where we can make sense of it. Multicultural relations offer the perfect stimulus to take us to our next evolutionary stage, key to our survival. Intercultural interactions and experiences provide an opportunity to integrate disciplines as well as ethnic and cultural views into our lives... we have here our own private social sciences laboratory.

In an attempt to integrate knowledge modern Western civilizations had to go to the Far East to 'rediscover' concepts of mindfulness, meditation and self-observation before arriving at the same conclusions the East had already arrived at: that it is not always easy to be tolerant or to go beyond our own mental borders. Becoming conscious of our own preconceived ideas of another's culture is a step in the right direction to our psychological, and even spiritual, evolution as a species. How the Brazilian culture can contribute to this process remains to be seen. The recent interest from business in emerging markets has opened many doors for inspired intercultural interaction. It is a delight to be part of the ongoing 'rediscovery' of Brazil where intensive social changes are taking place. Hopefully those changes will help our society achieve its full potential for growth and become a more fair and peaceful place. Even with the troubles of the past, the Brazilian door remains open for foreigners who dare to see beyond stereotypes.

Chapter 8

Epilogue

Chapter 8: Epilogue

My life has been blessed with the opportunity to be globally mobile, but for many years I could not make sense of these experiences and the impact they have had in my personal meaning-making process. The place from which I come (Brazil), the direction in which I moved, and the cultures I met along the way (in the US, Europe and, recently, China) somehow make more sense now – there is almost a synchronicity to it, as if the sequence was driven by my own developmental needs. It has often been painful, but always stimulating. It forced me to experience cultures as unique, but also as parts of a whole. Sharing my experience with friends and colleagues, many of whom were placed on the same path by coincidence, also added power to my humble intentions behind writing this book.

Outside my window in the Statsblibliotek (national library) in Malmo, Sweden, where I currently live, I have an opportunity to experience an imperfect but advanced Swedish society in which silence, social order, and mutual respect seem to represent the ideal. Often though, I find myself longing for the warm 'chaotic' noise, where disorder and inequality bring out the best and worst of people. I long for people's relaxed personal spaces, which I am welcome to enter.

Deep inside, something tells me there must be a reason why I listened to the gentle wind that whispered, "Follow me". My curiosity and my need to explore the world would not leave me, not until I agreed to go on and move to the next place... places where I encountered the same kind of human beings, just covered in colourful layers of culture. They always prove wrong any preconceived ideas I might have had about them and seem to reflect my own vulnerability and (half visible, half invisible) self-image.

If I look back to the beginning of writing this book, the only thing I wanted to prove was that Brazil is more than most people think it to be. I soon realized I needed to do much more; I needed to rescue my own reputation as a Brazilian. In the first part of the journey it was fascinating to identify myself with the indigenous population of Brazil, the Amerindians, about whom I was (and still am) very ignorant, as most Brazilians are. It was reassuring to confirm my vague impression that there is a missing piece in the puzzle of the Brazilian national identity. I was surprised to learn that the indigenous population in Brazil was three times bigger than the population of Portugal in 1500, and that their societies were small but democratic, harmonious and egalitarian. I learned their leaders were expected to be as charismatic as those in our modern societies. That their leadership did not necessarily stay in the family (it was not hereditary) proved to be an anthropologically meaningful sign of social development. Novaes describes these societies as "freedom societies whose model is not archaic, but rather has a contemporaneous validity" (Donisete & Grupioni, 1998).

As opposed to the general Brazilian tendencies these egalitarian societies, I learned, demonstrate an advanced ideology of social equality. They are also sensible to something bigger and are fully connected to the environment. They have *ecological intelligence*. Their life values go far beyond materialistic interests. Their spirituality, search for simplicity, and wholeness convinced me. I certainly have many reasons to be proud of and honored by my heritage. "How could I have lived without realizing the importance of such an invisible influence in my life?" I have since wondered.

Later in my journey I felt the same about my Africans origins. I found myself wanting to talk to any dark-looking person I saw, to ask about their experience in Brazil, and also here in Sweden. Even though my skin colour is not very dark, being a foreigner and outsider in Europe, I feel too often discriminated against. I have become more empathic to how it feels to be constantly reminded of one's difference.

Revisiting the official and unofficial Brazilian history was often painful; I was amazed to realize the human capacity for selective memory, to remember only what is convenient. But somehow I have reemerged stronger and more confident about how incredible it is to descend from such resilient groups of people. Memories of my childhood playmate – who was resentfully given away by her family who were black and poor – often make me wonder how many other poorer families in Brazil continue to experience this hardship. The experience of being 'kind of adopted' into another family for financial reasons confirms the real ambivalent Brazilian reality. In this journey, identifying with the 'darker side' of my family pushed me inwards, and helped me get in touch with my deepest strength.

From the beginning to the end of this book, I knew I had to shed light on the flow of things, from the movement of divergent thoughts such as 'we are all different' to convergent thoughts such as 'we are all the same'; like breathing in and breathing out. I also had to explore the intercultural encounter, its nature and dynamics. I had to find a way to make sense of it. I had to make sense (in my heart) of the consequences of where I came from and where I was going. I just needed to give it a name.

The idea of viewing cultures from an outsider's perspective seemed nonsense and, in the last chapters of the book, it came back to mind

Chapter 8: Epilogue

as in the emergent cultural approach. The link between cause and consequence started to take form. One must look at the emergent cultures as a diverse group, but also as a group with relevant similarities. It appeared to be of significant importance in my search to understand the Brazilian culture in the current international context. Most of all, the concept of culture needed to be expanded, as did the concept of high context cultures (often used to describe the BRICS countries). My recent experience in China, where I was able to witness both similarities and differences between this country and Brazil, also played a role in this book as it confirmed that I *should* dare to compare the nuances of high context cultures. The need to explore the reasons why other factors, such as ideology and education, make such a big difference in the formation of these cultures also became obvious. It became clear what we have in common too: the unnecessary struggle to fit in.

The whole idea of culture becomes as dynamic as ever, especially as it changes depending on which cultures we are comparing. It is amazing to acknowledge that only by establishing the term BRICS, do these countries begin to feel as if they belong to the same community even if we share little historical background. One would expect the Latin American region to be much closer, but, as discussed in *Chapter 2: Brazil Within Latin America*, distance remains between the Portuguese and Spanish sides, despite increasing commercial exchanges. Nevertheless, the importance of the *observer* in the study of culture remains vital, since his/ her perspectives play a central role in understanding the individual challenges of intercultural interactions.

On the way to reinterpreting Brazil, it was necessary to acknowledge the popular soccer-carnival-and-girls-in-small-bikinis stereotype. Dealing with this was critical to the process of trying to construct alternative views and to fill in the gaps. It was also necessary to explore the legacy of our past to understand how today's family structure, aversion to laws and regulations, division of labour, and educational gap are not just 'national preferences'. They turned out to be just unfortunate consequences of the struggle to survive. For professionals and visitors in Brazil this legacy is commonly experienced, for it is deeply rooted in the Brazilian working mentality, in the communication style, and in our approach to time.

While painting a more honest picture of Brazil, I had to make peace with history, at least with the historically biased interpretation of Brazil, which led to such a distorted but commonly held national image. The contrasting image of a country of the rich and the poor, with *favelas* (or communities of working families), and their passion for soccer and carnival, is part of Brazil, but it is certainly not the whole. I hope this book has, at the very least, shed light on this basic idea. I hope it has added to the list of words usually associated with Brazil and, in so doing, created a richer vocabulary.

Glossary of Foreign Words

Ameríndia	The indigenous peoples who lived in the American continent before the arrival of the European.
Advaita	One of the two principal Vedantic schools, it means nondual or 'not two', this oneness is a fundamental quality of everything.
Ashtavakra Gita	Astavakra Gita is a short text on Advaita Vedanta, which systematically deals with the mystical experiences of the individual in his flight to the transcendental peace and bliss.
Afrodescendentes	African descendants.
Bhagavad-Gita	A philosophic dialogue that is a sacred Hindu text, found in the Mahabharata, one of the ancient Sanskrit epics, known as the 'yoga of knowledge'.
IBGE	The Brazilian Statistics Institution (Instituto Brazileiro de geografia e Estatistica).
Conquistadores	Spanish soldiers and explorers who led military expeditions in the Americas and captured land for Spain.
Cacique	A native Indian chief who has political influence, his position is not necessarily hereditary.
Cunhadismo	A term used to explain the indigenous way to incorporate an outsider into their community by 'in-lawism', or marrying one of their members.
Cabelo ruim'	Literally translated it means 'the bad hair' but refers to the African curly hair.

Caboclo	Descendants of white and indigenous people.
COIAB	The Brazilian Coordination of the Indigenous Organization of the Amazon (Coordenação das Organizações Indígenas da Amazonia Brasileira).
Extra Communitari	An Italian word for non-Europeans.
Favelas	Slum or recently defined as communities of working families.
Gente bonita	Literally translated it means the beautiful people, but in the Brazilian culture it refers to the people with European ethnic origins. It also refers to people from the middle and higher social classes in Brazil.
Gente feia	Literally translated it means the ugly people, but in the Brazilian culture it refers to the people with both indigenous, African or a mix of these ethnic origins. It also refers to people from the lower social classes in Brazil.
Gringo	The non-native, the foreigner. It originated from the Spanish word which meant 'foreigner traders'.
Hermanos	Brothers in Spanish, but in Portuguese it means nationals from the Latin American countries.
Jeitinho Brasileiro	The Brazilian way to accomplish something by circumventing rules or social conventions. It is a typically method of social manipulation whereby an individual can use emotional resources, blackmail, family ties, promises, rewards or money to obtain favors or to get an advantage.
Mata Atlântica	A terrestrial biome and region which extends along the Atlantic coast of Brazil from Rio Grande do Norte state in the north to Rio Grande do Sul state in the south, and inland as far as Paraguay and the Misiones Province of Argentina.
Mameluke	The descendants of white and indigenous people.

Glossary

Pardo   It refers to the nonwhite color, or a mix between white and black.

Sapa Inca   The Spanish word for the ruler of the Kingdom of Cusco and later, the Emperor of the Inca Empire.

Svenska Västindiska Kompaniet   Swedish West India Company.

Morenos   People of nonwhite color, or a mix between white and black.

Mulatos   People of nonwhite color, or a mix between white and black.

Senzala   The slave house where they lived together. It was located close to the main farm house during the slavery period in Brazil.

Statsblibliotek   The National Library of Sweden.

Bibliography

Preface McNulty, Y. (2012). 'Being dumped in to sink or swim': an empirical study of organizational support for the trailing spouse. *Human Resource Development International*. Vol. 15, No. 4, September 2012, 417–434.

Chapter 1 Barth, F. (1995). Ethnic Groups and Boundaries. *American Anthropologist*, Vol. 97, No. 4, December Ed.

Baumeister, R. F., and Bushman, B. J. (2008), *Social Psychology and Human Nature*. United States: Thomson Wadsworth, 226-227.

Bennett, M. J. (1993). Towards ethnorelativism: a developmental model of intercultural sensitivity. In R. M. Paige (Ed.), *Education for the intercultural experience* (2nd ed., pp. 21–71). Yarmouth, ME: Intercultural Press.

Bennett, M. J. (2004). Becoming interculturally competent. In J.S. Wurzel (Ed.) *Toward multiculturalism: A reader in multicultural education*. Newton, MA: Intercultural Resource Corporation.

Coleman, P. T.; Kugler, K.G.; Bui-Wrzosinska, L.; Novak, A.; and Vallancher, R. (2012). Getting down to basics: a situated model of conflict in social relations. *Negotiation Journal*. January Ed.

Cuddy et al. (2009). Stereotype content model across cultures: Towards universal similarities and some differences. *British Journal of Social Psychology*, 48, 1-33.

Emberling, G. (1997). Ethnicity in complex societies: archaeological perspectives. *Journal of Archaeological Research*, Vol. 5, No. 4.

Bibliography

Fiske, T. F. & Taylor, S. E. (2013). *Social cognition from brain to culture*. London: Sage. 2nd Ed.

Furtado, C. (1991), *Formação Econômica do Brasil*. 24th Ed. São Paulo: Editora Nacional.

Gigerenzer, G. (2007), *Gut feelings: shortcuts to better decision making*. London: Penguin Books.

Hall, E. T. (1976), *Beyond Culture*. Garden City, NY: Anchor Press.

Hofstede, G. and G.J. Hofstede (2005), *Cultures and Organizations: Software of the Mind*. New York: McGraw-Hill.

Ito, T. A., & Urland, G. R. (2003). Race and gender in the brain: eletrocortisal mearuses of attention to the race and gender of multiple categorizable individuals. *Journal of Personality and Social Psychology*, 85, 616-626.

Jenks, C. (2003), (Ed.) *Culture: Critical Concepts in Sociology*,Vol. 1. London: Routledge.

Lewis, R. (2006), *When Cultures Collide: Leading Across Culture*. 3rd Ed. Finland: WS Book Well.

Mannoni, 0. (1991), *Prospero and Caliban: The Psychology of Colonization*. Michigan: University of Michigan Press.

Mazlevski, M. Professor at IMD (International Institute of Management) MBA programs Professor at IMD's MBA program (http://www.imd.org).

McIver, R. M. (1926), *The Modern State*. Oxford: Oxford University Press pp. 319-337 in Jenks, C. (ed) (2003) *Culture: Critical Concepts in Sociology*. New York: Routledge.

Rana, J. S. (2014), *The 4Ps framework advance negotiation and influence strategies for global effectiveness*. North Charleston, SC, US: CreateSpace Independent Publishing Platform.

Schwarcz, L. K. M. (1993), *O Espetáculo das Raças*. São Paulo: Companhia das Letras.

Skidmore, T.E (2010), *Brazil: Five Centuries of Change*. Oxford: Oxford University Press.

Trompenaars, F., Hampden-Turner, C. (1997), *Riding the Waves of Culture*. NY: McGraw-Hill.

Chapter 2 Burkholder, M.A. and J. Lyman (2012), *Colonial Latin America*. Oxford: Oxford University Press.

Furtado, C. (1991), *Formação Econômica do Brasil*. [Economic Formation of Brazil]. 24th Ed. São Paulo: Editora Nacional.

Hall, E. T. (1976), *Beyond Culture*. Garden City, NY: Anchor Press.

Hofstede, G. and G.J. Hofstede (2005), *Cultures and Organizations: Software of the Mind*. New York: McGraw-Hill.

Tannenbaum, F. (1946), *Slave and Citizen*. Place: Beacon Press.

Trompenaars, F., Hampden-Turner, C. (1997), *Riding the Waves of Culture*. NY: McGraw-Hill.

Chapter 3 The session *Insights from an expert* (from page 48) refers to the personal opinion of Edson Luís Gomes (www.amerindian.com.br).

BBC website http://news.bbc.co.uk/2/hi/americas/1231075.stm, [accessed on 24 January 2012].

Burkholder, M. A. and J. Lyman (2012), *Colonial Latin America*. Oxford: Oxford University Press.

Cunha, M. C. (2012), *Índios no Brasil: História, Direitos e Cidadania*. 1st ed. São Paulo: Claro Enigma.

Clastres, P. (1974), *A Sociedade Contra o Estado*. São Paulo: Cosac & Naify.

Bibliography

COIAB – Coordenação das Organizações Indígenas da Amazônia Brasileira [Coordination of the Indigenous Organizations of the Brazilian Amazon] [accessed on 02 November, 2012].

Donisete and B. Grupioni (1998), *Índios no Brasil*. Rio de Janeiro: Global Editora.

Freire, J. R. B. (2009), Cinco idéias equivocadas sobre os Índios in Siss, A. & Monteiro, A., *Educação, Cultura e Relações Interétnicas*. Rio de Janeiro: Editora da UFRRJ.

Furtado, C. (1991), *Formação Econômica do Brasil*. 24th Ed. São Paulo: Editora Nacional.

Goleman, D. (1995), *Emotional Intelligence*. New York: Bantam.

Gomes, L. (2007), *1808: como uma rainha louca, um príncipe medroso e uma corte corrupta enganaram Napoleão e mudaram a história de Portugal e Brasil*. Rio de Janeiro: Planeta do Brasil.

Gomes, L. (2010), *1822: como um homen sábio, uma princesa triste e um escocês louco por dinheiro ajudaram D. Pedro a criar o Brasil – um país que tinha tudo a dar errado*. Rio de Janeiro: Nova Fronteira.

Grandin, G. (2010), *Fordlândia Ascensão e queda da cidade esquecida de Henry Ford na selva*. Rio de Janeiro: Rocco.

IBGE, Brasil: 500 anos de povoamento / IBGE, Centro de documentação e Disseminação de Informações. Rio de Janeiro: IBGE, 2000.

Levis-Strauss, C. (1952), *Raça e História*. Paris: UNESCO.

Mahbub, U.H. (1996), *Reflections on Human Development*. Oxford: Oxford University Press.

Monteiro, J. (1998), 'Article/chapter name' in L. Donisete and B. Grupioni, *Índios no Brasil*. Rio de Janeiro: Global Editora.

Neves, E. G. (2000) O Velho e o Novo na Arqueologia Amazônica. *Revista USP*. São Paulo, n.44, p. 86-111, December/ February Ed.

Ribeiro, D. (2000), *The Brazilian People: The Formation and Meaning of Brazil*. Miami: University Press of Florida.

Santos, R. V., Fry, P. H., Monteiro, S., Maio, M. C., Rodrigues, J. C., Rodrigues, L. B., and Pena, S. D. J. (2009), Color, Race, and Genomic Ancestry in Brazil: Dialogues between Anthropology and Genetics. *Current Anthropology*. Vol. 50, N. 6.

Schwarcz, L. K. M. (2013), Complexo de Zé Carioca: notas sobre uma identidade mestiça e malandra. *Antropologia IV*, April Ed.

Schröder, P. (1996), *Reflections on Human Development*. Oxford: Oxford University Press.

Sen, A. (1997), *On economic inequality* (expanded ed.). Oxford New York: Clarendon Press Oxford University Press.

Shang-sheng, C. (2009), *Imigrantes e Imigração Chinesa no Rio de Janeiro (1910-1990)*. Rio de Janeiro: Revista Eletrônica Boletim do TEMPO, Ano 4, 07, Rio, [accessed on 12 August 2014].

Chapter 4 Araújo, T.C.N, (1987), *A classificação de "cor" nas pesquisas do IBGE* [The classification of color in the IBGE surveys]. Vol. 63, November 1987.

Bergad, L. W. (2007), *The Comparative Histories of Slavery in Brazil, Cuba, and the United States*. New York: Cambridge University Press.

Burkholder, M.A. and J. Lyman (2012), *Colonial Latin America*. Oxford: Oxford University Press.

Freyre, G. (1964), *The Masters and the Slaves: A Study in the Development of Brazilian Civilization*. New York: Random House.

Gomes, L. (2010), *1822: Como Um Homem Sábio, Uma Princesa Triste E Um Escocês Louco Por Dinheiro Ajudaram D. Pedro A Criar O Brasil – Um País Que Tinha Tudo A Dar Errado*. Rio de Janeiro: Nova Fronteira.

Gomes, L. (2013), *1889: Como um Imperador Cansado, um Marechal Vaidoso E Um Professor Injustiçado Contribuíram Para O Fim Da Monarquia E A Proclamação Da Republica No Brasi*. São Paulol: Nova Fronteira.

Grinberg, K. (2001), *Código Civil e Cidadania*. Rio de Janeiro: Jorge Zahar.

Madsen, M.B. (2012), 'Denmark cannot apologize for slave trade' in *Science Nordic*, 27 August, 2012.

Mattoso, Katia M. de Queirós (1996), *To Be a Slave in Brazil: 1550–1888*. Minnesota: Rutgers University Press.

Munanga, K. (2012), Nosso racismo é um crime perfeito. *Revista Fórum* http://revistaforum.com.br/blog/2012/02 / nosso-racismo-e-um-crime-perfeito [accessed in January 2015].

Petrucelli, J.L. (2007), *A Cor Denominada*. Rio de Janeiro: LPP/UERJ.

Popkin, R.H. (1966), *The Philosophy of the Sixteenth and Seventeenth Centuries*. NY: The Free Press.

Prandi, R. (2000), De africano a afro-brasileiro: etnia, identidade, religião. *Revista USP*. São Paulo, n.46, 52–65.

Rinchon, D. P. (1946), in F. Tannenbaum *Slave and Citizen*. Boston: Beacon Press.

Sussman, P., 'Timely regrets: Britain's guilt for its slave trade history' in *CNN International*, November 27, 2006 [accessed on Jan. 27th 2015].

Schwartzman, S. (1999), Fora De Foco: Diversidade E Identidades Étnicas No Brasil, *Novos Estudos*, CEBRAP. Nov. Ed.

Skidmore, T. E. (1974), *Black into White: Race and Nationality in Brazilian Thought*. New York: Oxford University Press.

Skytte, G. (1986), *Det Kungliga Svenska Slaveriet* [The Royal Swedish Slave Trade]. Stockholm: Askelin & Hägglund.

Tannenbaum, F. (1946), *Slave and Citizen*. Boston: Beacon Press.

The Daily Herald (2013). 'Dutch Parliament debates on slavery past, formal apology', [retrieved April 22, 2015, from http://thedailyherald.com/index.php?option=com_content&view=article&id=40356:dutch-parliament-debates-on-slavery-past-formal-apology&catid=1:islands-news&Itemid=54].

Trinkley, M. (2007), Growth of South Carolina's slave population. *South Carolina Information Highway*. [accessed April 22, 2015, from http://www.sciway.net/afam/slavery/population.html].

Williams, T. (2000), *The Homestead Act: A Major Asset-building Policy in American History*. Washington: Center for Social Development, Washington University.

Chapter 5 Bowlby, J. (1988), *A Secure Base: Parent-Child Attachment and Healthy Human Development*. New York: Basic Books.

Freyre, G. (1998), *Casa-Grande & Senzala*. Rio de Janeiro: Editora Record.

Graham, R. et al. (1991), *The Idea of race in Latin America, 1870-1940*. Missouri: Afro Hispanic Institute, Vol. 10, No. 1, 34-36.

Gomes, L. (2010), *1822: Como Um Homem Sábio, Uma Princesa Triste E Um Escocês Louco Por Dinheiro Ajudaram D. Pedro A Criar O Brasil – Um País Que Tinha Tudo A Dar Errado*. Rio de Janeiro: Nova Fronteira.

Gomes, L. (2013), *1889: Como um Imperador Cansado, um Marechal Vaidoso E Um Professor Injustiçado Contribuíram Para O Fim Da Monarquia E A Proclamação Da Republica No Brasi*. São Paulol: Nova Fronteira.

Mattoso, K. M. Q. (1996), *To Be a Slave in Brazil: 1550–1888*. Minnesota: Rutgers University Press.

Oxford English Dictionaries – Dictionary, Thesaurus, & Grammar, (n.d.).

Ribeiro, D. (2000), *The Brazilian People: The Formation and Meaning of Brazil*. Miami: University Press of Florida.

Skidmore, T.E (2010), *Brazil: Five Centuries of Change*. Oxford: Oxford University Press.

Chapter 6   Brown, B. (2012), *Daring Greatly*. NY: Gotham Books.

Csikszentmihalyi, M. (1988), 'The flow experience and its significance for human psychology' in Csikszentmihalyi, M., *Optimal Experience: Psychological Studies of Flow in Consciousness*. Cambridge: Cambridge University Press, 15–35.

Csikszentmihalyi, M. (1997), *Finding Flow*. New York: Basic Books.

FGV (2014), *Relatório ICJBrasil* 3o. e 4°. Trimestre. FGV Direito. Ano 6.

Grondin, S. (Ed.) (2008), *Psychology of time*. Bingley: Emerald.

Hall, E. T. (1976), *Beyond Culture*. Garden City, NY: Anchor Press.

Hofstede, G., G.J Hofstede, and M. Minkov (2010), *Cultures and organizations: software of the mind: intercultural cooperation and its importance for survival*. NY: McGraw Hill.

McCauley, C., & Van Velsor, E. (2004), *Handbook of leadership development*. San Francisco, CA: Jossey-Bass.

(PNUD) Programa das Nações Unidas para o Desenvolvimento (2010), *Valores e Desenvolvimento Humano 2010 / Programa das Nações Unidas para o Desenvolvimento*. Brasília, Brazil.

Trompenaars, F., Hampden-Turner, C. (1997), *Riding the Waves of Culture*. NY: McGraw-Hill.

Weiner, E., (2008), *Geography of Bliss: One Grump's Search for the Happiest Places in the World*. NY: Hachette Book Group.

Zakay D., Experiencing time in daily life. *The Psychologist*. August 2013, Vol. 25, 8.

Chapter 7

Allport, G. W. (1954), *The Nature of Prejudice*. Reading, MA: Addison-Wesley.

Bennett, M. J. (1993), Towards ethnorelativism: a developmental model of intercultural sensitivity. In R. M. Paige (Ed.), *Education for the intercultural experience* (2nd ed., pp. 21–71). Yarmouth, ME: Intercultural Press.

Coleman, P.T.; Kugler, K.g.; Bui-Wrzosinska, L.; Nowak, A.; Vallacher, R. (2012), Getting down to basics: a situated Model of conflict in social relations. *Negotiation Journal*. Jan. ed., 7-43

Hall, E. and G.L. Trager (1953), *The Analysis of Culture*. Washington: American Council of Learned Societies.

Henrich, J., Heine, S. J. & Norenzayan, A. (2010), The weirdest people in the world? *Behavioural and Brain Sciences*, 33 (2-3), 61-83.

Hofstede, G. and G.J. Hofstede (2005), *Cultures and Organizations: Software of the Mind*. New York: McGraw-Hill.

Kellert, Stephen R. (1993), Attitudes, Knowledge, and Behavior Toward Wildlife Among the Industrial Superpowers: United States, Japan, and Germany. *Journal of Social Issues* 49 (1):53-72.

Latin American Subaltern Studies Group (n.d.) "Founding Statement." Boundary 2. 20.3 (1993): 110-121. Duke University Press [accessed April 22, 2015 from http://www.jstor.org/stable/303344]

Montgomery, H. (1994). Towards a perspective theory of decision making and judgment. *Acta Psychologica*, 87, 155-178.

Trompenaars, F., Hampden-Turner, C. (1997), *Riding the Waves of Culture*. NY: McGraw-Hill.

Watters, E. (2013). We aren't the world: the weirdest people in the world. [retrieved on March 2014 from http://www.psmag.com/magazines/magazine-feature-story-magazines/joe-henrich-weird-ultimatum-game-shaking-up-psychology-economics-53135/].

About the Author

Successive international relocations throughout her adult life (both alone and with her family) have been a constant source of personal and professional growth for Simone Torres Costa.

Her interest in the long-term impact of expatriation on both executive performance and family relations begins with her own journey to the USA, Sweden, Poland and Italy. After 15 years abroad, she moved back to Brazil, where she co-wrote the book *The Mission of Detective Mike: Moving Abroad* (Summertime Publishing, 2010), and 'rediscovered' her interest in the Brazilian culture.

Being part of an international network of intercultural professionals has also added great value to her work in the past few years, especially when coaching executives focused on their global leadership development. Her coaching and training of international leaders offered the amazing opportunity to apply both her business and psychology background. It has also taught her about the reality of the organizations' intercultural challenges and how to connect theory and practice.

Simone chose a multidisciplinary educational pathway, from a business background (MBA from Lund University, Sweden) to a psychology degree from The Open University in Milan, Italy. She is a member of the British Psychological Society and is an ICF-certified coach. Currently she is taking her Master's in Psychology at Lund University.

Simone can be contacted via:

Email: simone_tce@interculturalplus.com

Website: www.interculturalplus.com

LinkedIn: https://br.linkedin.com/in/interculturalplus